JO VERSO'S
COMPLETE
CROSS STITCH
COURSE

JO VERSO'S
COMPLETE
CROSS STITCH
COURSE

Reader's Digest

THE READER'S DIGEST ASSOCIATION, INC.
Pleasantville, New York/Montreal

DEDICATION

To Jill de Florin, first a pupil, now a friend.

A READER'S DIGEST BOOK

Edited and produced by David & Charles Publishers
Art Director: Brenda Morrison
Commissioning Editor: Cheryl Brown
Edited by Lin Clements
Designed by Design Revolution
Designer: Margaret Foster
Chartist and Illustrator: Ethan Danielson
Hand model: Jane Trollope
Step-by-step photography: Alan Duns
Styled photography: David Johnson
Stylist: Kit Johnson

First published in the UK in 1996

Library of Congress Cataloging in Publication Data

Verso, Jo.
   [Complete cross stitch course]
   Jo Verso's complete cross stitch course.
      p. cm.
   Includes index.
   ISBN 0-89577-943-9
   1. Cross-stitch. 2. Cross-stitch—Patterns.
TT778.C76V43   1997
746.46—dc20   96-41819

Printed in Great Britain

CONTENTS

✕ ✕ ✕ ✕ ✕

INTRODUCTION

When I embarked on my first piece of counted cross stitch embroidery 18 years ago I had only vague memories of working cross stitches on a Binca mat at school. I thought that there was nothing to it and that providing I formed the crosses in the correct positions all would be well. This rudimentary approach does work, but I soon discovered that there were many ways of tackling the various techniques, some more successful than others. This led me to the library to see what the experts had to say on the subject. I found snippets of information, but nowhere was there a comprehensive guide. By dint of sifting through many books and much practical experience I have discovered that counted cross stitch is very simple to produce badly, but that with a little know-how and care a much better and more satisfying result can be achieved.

Would you like to take up cross stitch embroidery but are unsure as to how to start and what to buy? Are you baffled by the terms Aida and evenweave? Do you know the difference between Linda and Jobelan? Should you work with embroidery floss or flower thread? This book will answer all your questions, demystify all the jargon, and simplify each step of learning to cross stitch. It will take you step by step through all the stages to proficiency so that after completing the last chapter you will be able to tackle any cross stitch project with complete confidence.

When I was a beginner I bought a whole bolt of embroidery fabric in a sale thinking that I had found a real bargain, only to realize later that it was not an evenweave and therefore not suitable for cross stitch. It glowers at me from the corner of my workroom to this day. Another white elephant was the pair of so-called embroidery scissors whose points proved to be unsuitable for unpicking fine work. The materials and equipment needed to start cross stitch embroidery are illustrated and explained to help you avoid such costly mistakes before you start stitching. Everything you are likely to come across is covered, from absolute essentials to items that are nice to have but not strictly necessary.

Each chapter is devoted to a new skill or stitching technique, and a specially designed project has been provided to enable you to master the skill in question. By working the project not only will you learn and practice the technique, you'll also end up with a delightful creation for your efforts. For example, it would be very tedious to work 100 French knots on a piece of scrap fabric when learning this stitch, only to discard the work on completion. By stitching the Lavender Sachet Bag

design on page 52, not only will you stitch 100 French knots, enough to give you a lot of practice, you will also end up with a decorative and useful item.

Throughout the skill chapters, particularly in the early techniques, you will find page references in parentheses after specific steps. These indicate that you can turn back to that page to review what you have already learned.

To get you started there is a needle case to stitch that will teach you the first basic skill—the full cross stitch. As a bonus you will make a pretty and practical holder for your cross stitch needles. Other projects will produce gifts and mementos that can be put to good use, so while you are learning, none of your stitching goes to waste. After working from basic skills through advanced techniques you will have gained the confidence to tackle any future cross stitch project that takes your fancy.

Each chapter builds on the skills learned in previous chapters and step-by-step photography is used lavishly so you will feel that your teacher is with you every step of the way: seeing as well as reading how to do something always makes the lesson easier to grasp. One in ten people is left-handed, but cross stitch embroidery need hold no terrors for such stitchers. Although the techniques in the book are demonstrated by a right-handed

stitcher, holding a small handbag mirror next to an illustration will reverse the image. Sitting opposite a right-handed stitching friend can also be very helpful.

While cross stitch is a simple form of embroidery, accessible to anyone who can count, it is equally simple to produce poor stitching. Even the most proficient of us can always improve our work; so, after acquiring the basic skills, it is desirable to hone and perfect them. In sections called "An Expert's Secret," which appear throughout the book, you will find hints and tips to help you achieve the best possible result.

Until now there has been no book devoted completely to the subject of cross stitch techniques. Most cross stitch books offer a "Techniques" section but fill the majority of their pages with tempting designs. No two books offer the same information, and you may have to consult many publications to get answers to all your questions. In this single volume you will find the knowledge gleaned from my many years of professional involvement in the cross stitch world plus countless hours of cross stitching for profit and, above all, pleasure. With this book, beginners and experienced stitchers alike can discover the delight and satisfaction of working cross stitch projects, confident that they are using the correct materials and the best possible techniques.

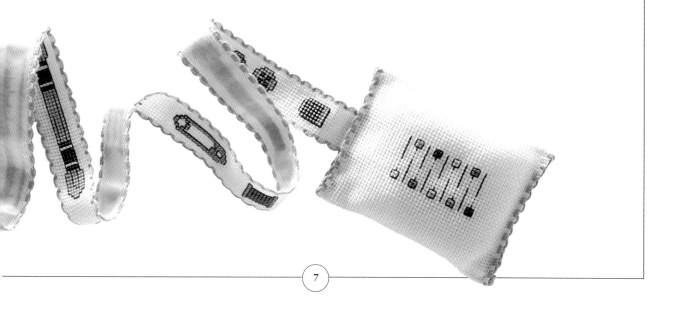

MATERIALS & EQUIPMENT

*Before you can get started you will
need to assemble some basic supplies.
Photographed on the following pages are many of the
most readily available materials, but you will
probably never use the full range offered. Each skill
in the book will list the specific materials required
to work the project.*

FABRICS

On entering a good needlecraft shop you will find a bewildering array of embroidery fabrics. Disregard the canvas section: canvas is used for needlepoint and canvas work. Look for the Aida and evenweave fabrics on which cross stitch is worked.

Cross stitch fabrics are classified either by a thread count number, i.e., how many threads or blocks there are to 1in (2.5cm), or by an HPI (holes per inch) number, i.e., how many holes there are to 1in (2.5cm). These two terms are the same and will tell you how many cross stitches to 1in (2.5cm) you will work on the fabric. The lower the count, the coarser the fabric and the larger the cross stitch will be. Conversely, the higher the count, the finer the fabric and the smaller the cross stitch will be.

Each design in this book tells you which fabric to work on and how much is needed, but if a pattern in another publication gives you no guidance and you are bewildered by the choice of fabrics, choose a fabric that suits your pocketbook, feels good to handle, and has a thread count that is not too fine for your eyesight.

Aida Fabric
Aida, produced by Permin and Zweigart, is a widely available cotton fabric in which threads are packed together during the weaving process to form blocks.

These blocks form easy-to-see squares and each cross stitch is worked over one block. The coarsest is 6-count Binca, which is cut into squares mainly for children. Other Aida fabrics come in various colors and counts – 8, 11, 14, 16, and 18 HPI, or blocks, to 1in (2.5cm), being most common.

Some Aidas are shot with metallic thread, such as Lurex, to add sparkle to special occasions and some, like Rustico, are flecked to give a rustic appearance. Easy-count Aida has a contrasting thread woven into it at regular intervals to assist counting; when work is complete this thread is easily removed without any disturbance to the stitching.

Damask fabrics, for tablecloths and pillows, are available with areas of Aida woven into them at regular intervals. Aida bands or ribbons come in a variety of widths with plain or decorative edges; when stitched, these have many uses and can decorate a multitude of household items.

Aida can be bought by the yard or, often, as small offcuts. By being readily available and having holes that are easy to see and count, it is an ideal fabric for beginners.

Opposite *The count of the fabric determines the size of the design, as these Aida samples show.*

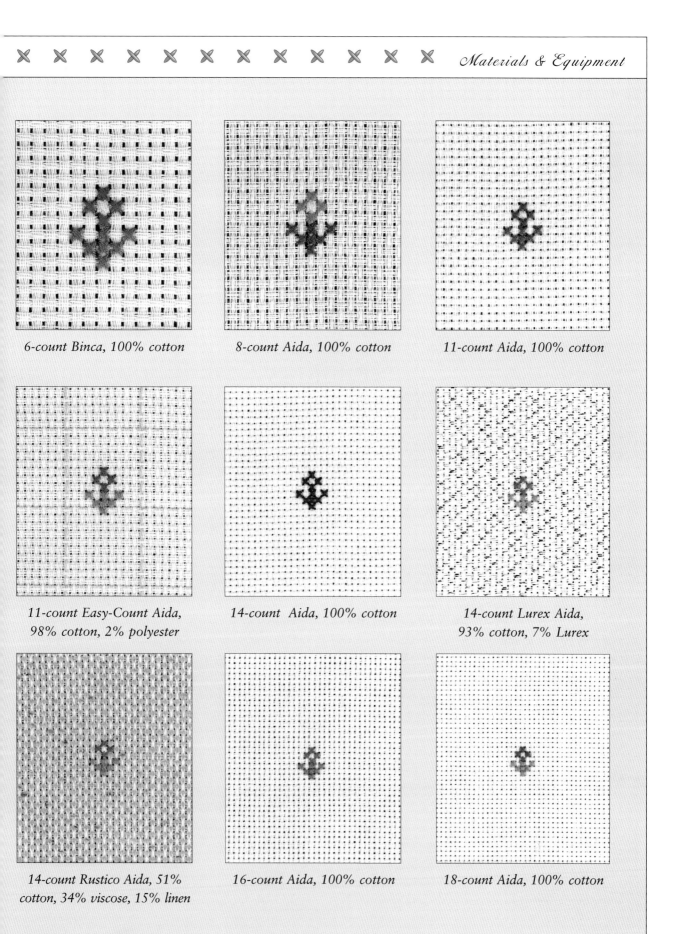

6-count Binca, 100% cotton

8-count Aida, 100% cotton

11-count Aida, 100% cotton

11-count Easy-Count Aida,
98% cotton, 2% polyester

14-count Aida, 100% cotton

14-count Lurex Aida,
93% cotton, 7% Lurex

14-count Rustico Aida, 51%
cotton, 34% viscose, 15% linen

16-count Aida, 100% cotton

18-count Aida, 100% cotton

A selection of Aida and evenweave bands.

Evenweave Fabric

Evenweave fabric is woven with single threads and is called evenweave because there are the same number of weft (horizontal) threads as there are warp (vertical) threads to 1in (2.5cm). Fabric that is not evenweave will become distorted as you stitch it and is therefore unsuitable. When using an evenweave fabric the cross stitch is worked over two threads, so an evenweave with 20 threads to 1in (2.5cm) will produce 10 cross stitches to 1in (2.5cm). There are many thread counts available in evenweave and a large choice of colors.

Common evenweaves are Zweigart Linda (cotton) and Jobelan (cotton/viscose mix), but the Rolls Royce of evenweave fabrics is evenweave linen with its excellent qualities of durability and handling. Permin makes a large range of evenweave linens, and Zweigart produces the popular Dublin, Belfast, and Edinburgh linens.

As evenweave linen is woven from natural fibers, some of the threads are coarser than others, but by working the cross stitch over two threads any discrepancies are evened out.

Zweigart Oslo is also available. This is a Hardanger fabric that is ideal for beginners owing to its low thread count but appearance of a fine fabric. This is because Hardanger fabrics are double rather than single weave, so the cross stitch is worked over two pairs of threads.

Other Materials

The projects in this book will give you the chance to work with various materials as follows. **Plastic canvas** can be cut and assembled into three-dimensional objects. **Perforated paper,** for delicate work, can be folded and cut without the edges fraying. **Aida Plus** is like perforated paper but less fragile. **Waste canvas** can be applied to almost any fabric to make it suitable for cross stitching. **Silk gauze** allows for very fine work in miniature.

Opposite *Various evenweave fabric counts.*

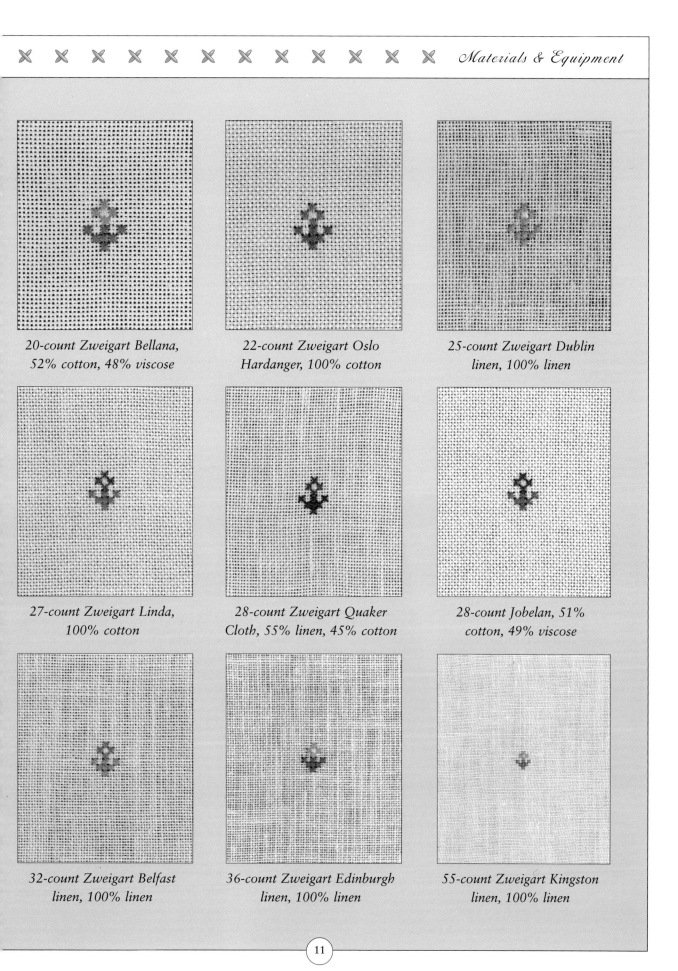

20-count Zweigart Bellana,
52% cotton, 48% viscose

22-count Zweigart Oslo
Hardanger, 100% cotton

25-count Zweigart Dublin
linen, 100% linen

27-count Zweigart Linda,
100% cotton

28-count Zweigart Quaker
Cloth, 55% linen, 45% cotton

28-count Jobelan, 51%
cotton, 49% viscose

32-count Zweigart Belfast
linen, 100% linen

36-count Zweigart Edinburgh
linen, 100% linen

55-count Zweigart Kingston
linen, 100% linen

Calculating How Much Fabric to Buy

You will need a piece of fabric large enough to accommodate your stitched design, with enough spare fabric all round the edges to allow at least 2in (5cm) for turning when the embroidery is framed or made up.

To calculate the fabric size, first take the stitch count or find it by counting the number of squares horizontally and vertically on your design. Then divide the number of squares by the number of cross stitches produced per inch (2.5cm) of your chosen fabric.

For example:

Your design has 110 squares by 99.

Your chosen fabric is 11-count Aida, so you will get 11 cross stitches to 1in (2.5cm).

110 divided by 11 = 10.

99 divided by 11 = 9.

Your finished embroidery will measure 10 x 9in (25.5 x 23cm) and to this you need to add a turning allowance of 2in (5cm) all round. Therefore the piece of fabric you need to cut should measure 14 x 13in (35.5 x 33cm).

Remember to divide the thread count of an evenweave fabric by 2 to arrive at the number of cross stitches per 1in (2.5cm): for example, a 28 count evenweave will produce 14 cross stitches per 1in (2.5cm).

To check whether your embroidery will fit a chosen mount, for example when working a greeting card, calculate the finished size of the embroidery as described above. If it is too large to fit the mat opening, work on a finer fabric with a higher count. If it is too small, work on a coarser fabric with a lower count.

THREADS

There is a large range of threads available for cross stitching today and the thoughtful choice of color and type of thread can enhance a piece of work greatly.

Embroidery Floss

This is the most commonly used thread for working counted cross stitch onto the background fabric. DMC, Anchor, and Madeira all produce excellent embroidery floss in every color imaginable. Embroidery floss is bought by the skein, each skein containing 9yd (8.25m) of mercerized six-stranded floss. It is easiest to work with an 18in (45cm) length cut from the skein. Single strands can then be removed to form groups of two, three, or more strands, as required, to achieve many different effects.

Flower Threads

Flower threads, produced by DMC and the Danish Handcraft Guild, are made from 100 percent cotton and are nondivisible. Whereas embroidery floss has a lustrous finish, flower thread has a matte finish and is suitable when a softer effect might be desired.

Metallic Thread

Metallic thread can be used to add glitter and interest to the embroidery. DMC produces a range of soft metallic threads suitable for cross stitch embroidery. Blending filament is ideal for projects that require a lot of sparkle.

Many threads are set out to tempt you in a needlework shop. Crewel wools are not used for traditional cross stitch embroidery, but rules were made to be broken and interesting experiments can be made when you are feeling more adventurous. Different threads, such as Marlitt and pearl cotton, will produce different effects, so do not reject a thread until you have tried working a few stitches with it.

How Many Strands of Thread?

Usually the pattern you are working will tell you how many strands of thread you should be working with—that is, sufficient to give good coverage of the fabric but not so many that they will distort the holes. As a general rule, for 10–13 cross stitches to 1in (2.5cm) use three strands of floss. For 14–18 cross stitches to 1in (2.5cm) use two strands of floss. Backstitch and French knots are generally worked with one strand only. If in doubt, try a few sample stitches in the corner of your fabric to check coverage.

CROSS STITCHER'S TOOLS

The following equipment is essential for counted cross stitch. Buy the best quality you can afford; treat your investment with care and it should last for many years.

Tapestry Needles

Use a blunt tapestry needle that slips easily through the holes in your fabric without piercing or splitting the threads. Finer needles have a higher number on the packet (26, 24); thicker needles have lower numbers (22, 18).

To embellish cross stitch with beads, attach these using a beading needle. These are also available in different sizes but are finer and have a sharp point.

Embroidery Scissors

You will need sharp, fine-pointed scissors to cut lengths of embroidery floss from the skein and to trim off finished threads on the back of the work. To preserve their sharpness, never cut fabric or paper with them—scissors that are not sharp enough will chew the thread and make a mess. Wear your scissors on a ribbon around your neck to keep them always at hand.

Embroidery and Flexi-Hoops

These are used to hold the fabric taut while stitching and are necessary to produce even stitching. Use a hoop only if the area to be stitched fits easily inside it. If the hoop has to be moved over existing embroidery, the stitches risk being distorted by the pressure of the hoop.

Dressmaking Scissors

You will need these to cut your fabric to size before sewing.

Sewing Thead

This is used to overcast the edges of your fabric to prevent fraying. It is also used to baste the central lines on the fabric. Do not be tempted to use dark-colored sewing thread for basting as it can leave slight traces of fibers to discolor your fabric.

Thread Organizer

Keep spare strands of embroidery thread on a thread organizer to keep them in order. You can make your own by punching holes down the side of a piece of lightweight cardboard, such as from inside a package of tights.

Embroidery Frames

These are designed for pieces of work that are too large to fit into embroidery hoops. They consist of two wooden stretchers at the side and two wooden rollers at the top and bottom, held in place with wing nuts or pegs. The rollers each have a piece of webbing fixed to them onto which the fabric is stitched.

Useful but Not Crucial Equipment

The following equipment can be acquired as and when you wish, or put your chosen items on your Christmas list.

• *Unpicking scissors* have a neat little hook in the bottom blade that assists the removal of offending threads.

• *Table or floor-standing frames* allow you to have one hand at the front of the work and one at the back, speeding up work considerably.

• *Gold-plated needles* are sheer self-indulgence for some but a boon for those whose body chemistry removes the plating from an ordinary tapestry needle.

• *Stitching gloves* prevent the hands from getting tired as you stitch.

• *A stitch catcher* is a nifty little gadget that allows you to use even the last tiny piece of thread before it runs out.

• *Needle threaders* are useful if your eyesight isn't great and there is nobody around to thread the needle for you.

• *A work stand* allows you to clamp a hoop or frame to it, leaving both hands free to work.

• *Chart holders* are magnetic boards used in conjunction with magnetic chart markers to help you keep your place on a chart.

• *Daylight bulbs* can be used in most lamps to give a good light for stitching at night or on dull days.

• *Magnifiers* can keep us stitching happily when eyesight is failing. They range from a pair of strong spectacles to floor-standing magnifiers with built-in lights. Line magnifiers can be placed over charts to make them easier to read. Magnifiers are available that hang around your neck or clip onto your existing spectacles. For cross stitch embroidery to be enjoyable, you have to be able to see what you are doing.

• *Shade cards*, available from thread manufacturers are invaluable if you progress to choosing your own shades of thread for projects. Colors are grouped into "families" of different depths of each shade; so if you want a light, medium, and dark blue that blend well, for example, choose them from a suitable blue family. You can see at a glance all available shades, which also assists choice.

GETTING STARTED

*Once you have assembled the materials for your
project, you will be eager to start stitching at once.
But do take time to set up the work correctly, as careful
preparation at this stage can make all the difference
to the quality of your finished masterpiece.*

PREPARING THE FABRIC

1 Cut the fabric to the size stated in the You Will
Need section of the project instructions. When
working designs from other books or magazines
and no size is stated, you must ensure that you have
allowed enough fabric for the design (p.12), plus
2in (5cm) all round to allow for mounting. When
cutting the fabric use sharp dressmaking scissors: do

not be tempted to use your embroidery scissors—
these should only be used to cut embroidery thread.
If possible, make a note of where the selvage edges
are on the fabric piece and aim to have these on the
left and right of the design as it is stitched, as this
will make the stretching of the finished piece a
little easier.

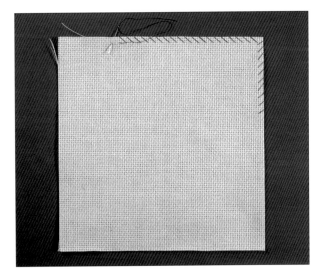

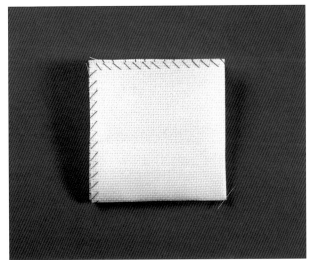

2 Overcast the edges of the fabric to prevent
fraying: this can be done by hand or on a
sewing machine using a zigzag stitch. Frayed
threads at the edge of the work can get tangled up
with embroidery thread on the back and are a
nuisance. Before you start to stitch, iron the fabric
to remove any stubborn creases.

3 Find the center of the fabric, as this is where the
first stitch will be worked. Stitching the central
stitch of a design in the center of the fabric ensures
that there will be an even amount of spare fabric all
around the design, which is important at the
mounting stage. Fold the fabric into four and mark
the central point temporarily with a pin.

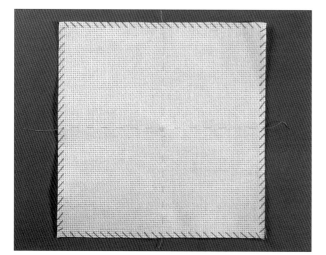

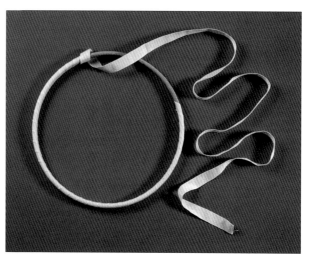

4 Using light-colored basting thread, mark the vertical and horizontal lines that meet in the center of the fabric. Remove the pin. Once the cross stitching is complete, the basting threads will be removed.

USING AN EMBROIDERY HOOP
(STEPS 5 – 7)

5 Mount the fabric in a hoop large enough to contain the whole design: moving a hoop around over existing stitches will crush and distort them. First, wrap the inner hoop with a white bias cotton tape to protect the fabric and prevent slipping.

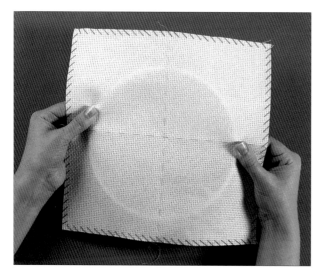

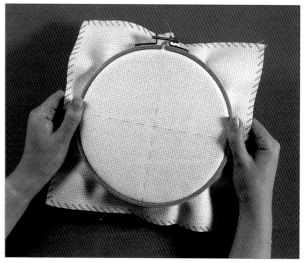

6 Lay the fabric over the inner ring of the hoop, positioning it so that the center of the fabric lies in the center of the ring.

7 Place the outer ring of the hoop over the inner ring, with the tension screw at the top, out of the way. Press the outer hoop down over the inner and tighten the tension screw, adjusting the fabric so that it is taut as a drum. Check that the horizontal and vertical threads have not been distorted in the process. Reposition the fabric if they have.

USING A FLEXI-HOOP

8 Flexi-hoops are circular or oval plastic hoops that consist of a rigid inner hoop and a flexible outer hoop. The outer hoop is eased onto the inner hoop to hold work tautly in place. Flexi-hoops come in a variety of sizes, colors, and finishes. Because they are available in very small sizes, they are often used instead of wooden embroidery hoops for working very small projects like the chatelaine pincushion (p. 48). When stitching is finished, the flexi-hoop can be used as a decorative frame for the completed work (see Exploring the Options, p. 110).

USING AN EMBROIDERY FRAME
(STEPS 9 – 11)

9 If the design you are working is too large to fit a hoop, use an embroidery frame. First, hem your fabric to strengthen the edges so that it will not pull apart when it is laced to the frame.

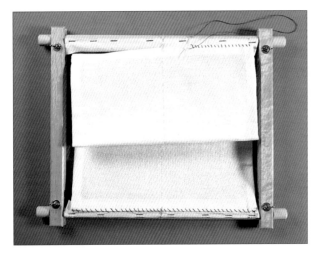

10 Sew the top of the fabric to the top piece of the frame's webbing, and do the same at the bottom, matching the center of the fabric to the center of the webbing. Do not be tempted to use thumbtacks or staples to attach the fabric—threads may be pulled, which will ruin the fabric.

11 Lace the sides of the fabric to the frame stretchers with strong thread and, when both sides are laced, tighten the threads and the wing nuts so that the fabric is stretched taut. Tie the ends of the threads firmly to the stretchers. When working a long design it may be necessary to roll completed stitching onto one of the rollers to expose more fabric for work. In this case, a sheet of white tissue paper rolled into the back of the work will prevent crushing the stitches.

USING WASTE FABRIC (STEPS 12 – 13)

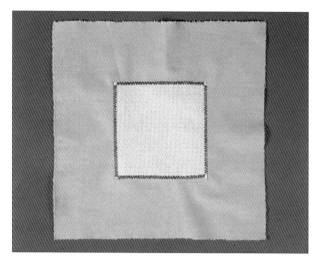

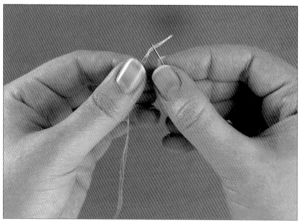

12 When working very tiny designs it can be wasteful to cut a piece of embroidery fabric large enough to fit a hoop. If this is the case, cut a piece of waste fabric large enough to fit the hoop. Cut a piece of embroidery fabric to the required size and stitch this firmly to the center of the waste fabric.

13 Cut away the waste fabric from behind the embroidery fabric. Turn the fabric to the right side and mount into a hoop as usual. When the embroidery is complete, trim away the remaining waste fabric and discard it.

THREADING THE NEEDLE (STEPS 14 – 15)

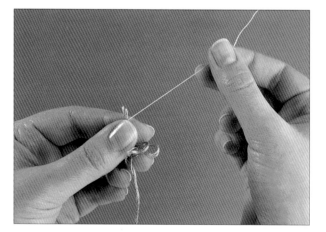

14 To thread the needle to begin stitching select the color indicated by the chart for the center of the design. Gently unwind an 18in (45cm) length from your skein of embroidery floss and cut it off. Remove the required number of strands from the cut length one at a time.

15 Lay the removed threads side by side and stroke them to remove any twists. The fewer twists you have on the thread, the better the stitches will cover the fabric. Thread the needle and you are ready to work your first cross stitch.

READING A CHART

Cross stitch designs are available where the pattern is printed directly onto the fabric and the cross stitches are worked to cover the printing. The resulting cross stitches tend to be uneven and rather hit-and-miss, so results can be disappointing. Far more popular now are designs for counted cross stitch, which is the subject of this book. Counted cross stitch is worked from charts, and each square on the chart, whether stitched or unstitched, represents one block of Aida or two threads of evenweave fabric. It is therefore important to understand a chart and be able to translate it into stitching.

All the charts in this book are printed in color so that you can see at a glance which color to use for each stitch. To help further, each colored square carries a symbol to clarify the exact color required. If two different shades of one color are used, the symbols help to distinguish between them. If you wish to make your work easier to carry with you, the symbols make it possible to take a black and white photocopy of a color chart which can then be colored in using crayons if you find this helpful. All the charts have a color key that tells you which

color thread corresponds to the colors marked on the chart.

It is important to find the central stitch in the chart, as this is the first stitch worked in the center of the fabric. Many charts will have arrows indicating the central point, others will mark the central point with an asterisk or other mark, such as the five-pointed star on my charts. If a chart is not marked in this way, find the center by counting the squares in each direction and dividing by 2. You can then mark the center for yourself.

You may have come across designs that have an unworked square or squares in the center. In this case, count the empty squares on the chart outward from the center to the first area of stitching indicated. On the fabric, count the same number of blank blocks/pairs of threads outward from the center to find the corresponding position to start stitching.

Opposite *This chart shows the various symbols used to indicate specific stitches.*
Below *This chart shows the use of a color key for threads used.*

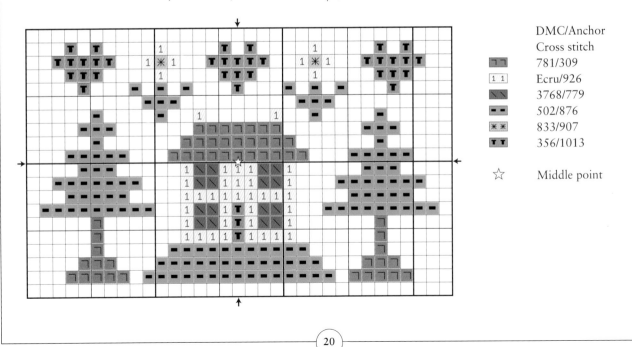

	DMC/Anchor Cross stitch
⅂⅂	781/309
1 1	Ecru/926
◥◣	3768/779
– –	502/876
✳ ✳	833/907
T T	356/1013
☆	Middle point

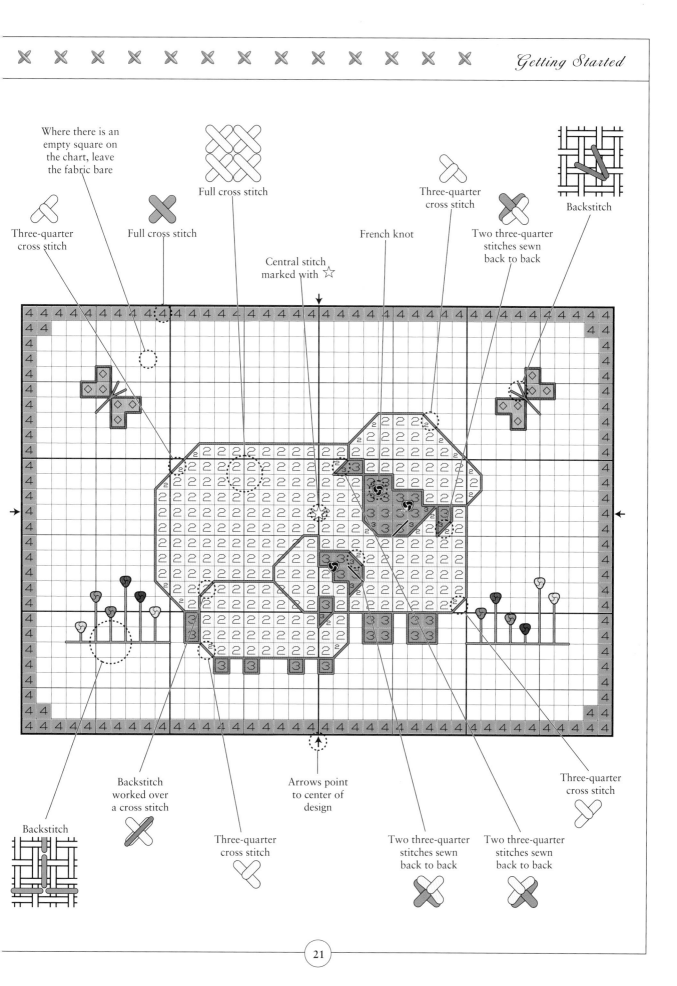

Where there is an empty square on the chart, leave the fabric bare

Full cross stitch

Three-quarter cross stitch

Backstitch

Three-quarter cross stitch

Full cross stitch

French knot

Two three-quarter stitches sewn back to back

Central stitch marked with ☆

Backstitch

Backstitch worked over a cross stitch

Three-quarter cross stitch

Arrows point to center of design

Two three-quarter stitches sewn back to back

Two three-quarter stitches sewn back to back

Three-quarter cross stitch

FULL CROSS STITCH

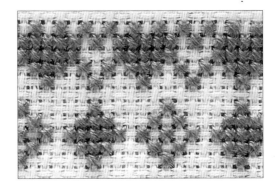

*he stitch that forms the basis of
counted cross stitch, and the one you will use
most frequently, is the full cross stitch. Crosses are formed
in two stages to produce a stitch that is square
in shape and corresponds to the squares on the graph
paper of your charted pattern.*

NEEDLE CASE

Finished Size: (folded) 4½ x 3¼in (11.5 x 8cm). Stitch Count: 57 x 37

Your first pattern has been designed so that the first row of cross stitches you work is a simple straight line. Each line thereafter requires a little more skill but builds on what you have just learned. The stitching is in a single color to ensure minimum outlay on materials and to allow you to concentrate on the stitches themselves. So that none of your effort is wasted, your first steps in cross stitch can be made into a useful and decorative needle case in which to keep your cross stitch needles. By changing the color of the background fabric and thread, a totally different effect can be achieved from the same design, as you can see by comparing the finished needle case pictured opposite with that on page 29.

You Will Need
- *7in (18cm) embroidery hoop*
- *11 x 11in (28 x 28cm) 11-count Aida fabric, in white or sky blue*
- *5½ x 4¼in (14 x 11cm) 11-count Aida fabric, in white or sky blue*
- *Embroidery floss in blue or white (see color key)*
- *Tapestry needle, size 24*
- *10 x 4¼in (25.5 x 11cm) cotton backing fabric*
- *White sewing thread*
- *30in (76cm) cotton lace or braid for trimming*
- *Short length of ⅛in (3mm) wide ribbon to make into a bow*
- *8½ x 3in (21.5 x 7.5cm) white felt*

1 Prepare the larger piece of Aida fabric for work (p. 16). Mount the fabric into the hoop (p. 17), then thread the needle (p. 19). Starting at the center of the chart, match it to the center of your fabric, which has already been marked with basting thread.

THE KNOTLESS START
(STEPS 2 – 6)
Use this method of starting when working with uneven numbers of strands of thread in the needle. It permits a flat, neat start without a bulging knot on the back of the work that can form an unsightly lump.

2 Though it sounds like a contradiction, tie a knot in the end of a three-stranded length of floss and insert the needle on the right side of the fabric

approximately 1½in (3.5cm) to the right of the center. Bring the needle up at the starting position (bottom left) of Row 1 marked ☆ on the chart.

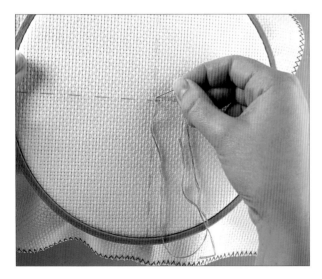

3 Insert the needle in the top right-hand hole of the block, thus forming half a cross stitch.

4 Bring the needle out at the bottom left-hand hole of the next block and insert it in the top right-hand hole of that block. Continue to form half crosses going from left to right (see diagram, left).

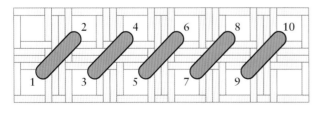

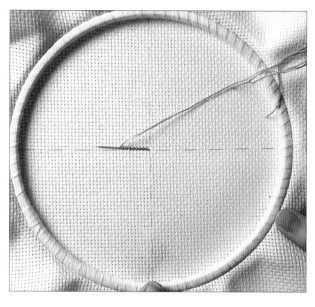

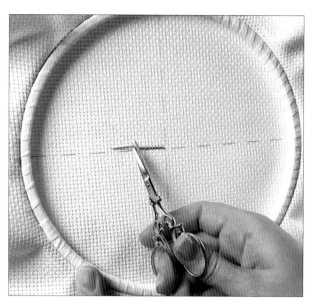

5 Continue this way, securing the knotted end of the thread on the back of the work as you go.

6 When the thread is secure, cut off the knot on the front of the work and trim the tail on the back.

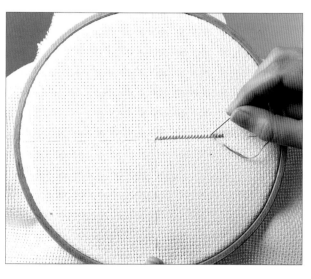

An Expert's Secret

Always work the first half of all full cross stitches in the same direction. This ensures that all top stitches will lie in the same direction, giving an even appearance and uniform sheen to the work. It does not matter whether your bottom stitch goes from bottom left to top right, or from bottom right to top left, so long as you are consistent. Beware of turning work in your hand, to work the side of a border, for instance—a large cross stitch worked in the corner of your fabric will serve as an instant reference.

7 Working from right to left, cross each stitch using the same holes as before, but stitching

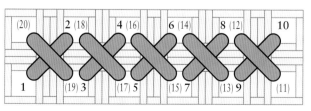

from bottom right to top left of each block. All cross stitches "hold hands" and share holes with their neighbors (see diagram, left). Finish Row 1 by stitching the remaining cross stitches that lie to the left of the starting position, ensuring all bottom stitches lie in the same direction.

THE KNOTLESS FINISH (STEPS 8 – 9)
This method finishes a thread neatly, avoiding unsightly knots and lumps.

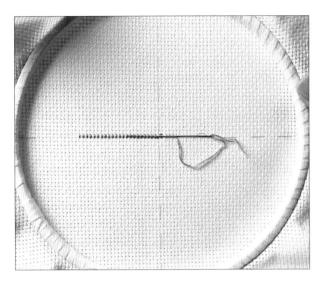

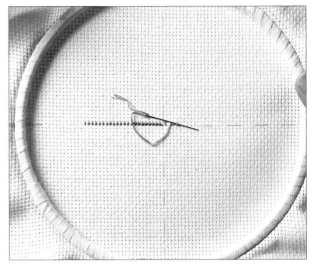

8 On the back of the fabric, thread the needle through the back of the last three stitches worked.

9 Return, jumping over one stitch and threading the needle through the back of two stitches. Trim the thread neatly, close to the stitching, using sharp embroidery scissors.

JOINING A NEW THREAD (STEPS 10 – 11)

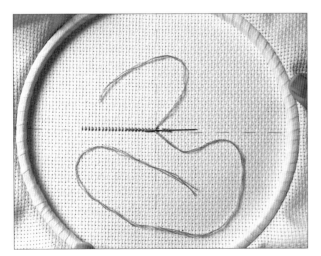

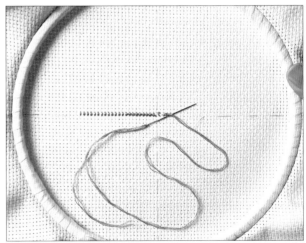

10 To join a new thread where there are existing stitches pass the needle through the back of three stitches on the back of the work as close as possible to where you want to start stitching again.

11 Take a backstitch into the last stitch to secure the thread and bring the needle to the front of the work. You are now ready to continue stitching. (Continued on p. 28.)

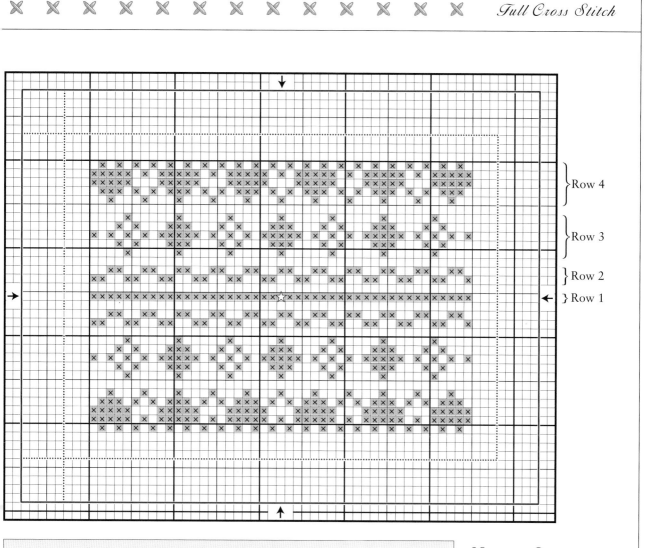

Row 4
Row 3
Row 2
Row 1

Emergency Unpicking Kit

Check frequently that your counting is correct; while one hesitates to mention the ghastly word "unpicking," it is something that has to be done by even the most proficient cross stitchers from time to time. To help avoid it, count your stitches carefully as you work, and recheck frequently as work progresses. The few minutes it takes are well spent and could save hours of work later. Never be tempted to use a stitch ripper, as this will pull and distort neighboring stitches. To make the task easier, equip yourself with a pair of unpicking scissors. The tiny hook at the end of the bottom blade allows the offending stitch to be lifted for cutting and removal. Tweezers can assist you to remove the threads, and transparent tape helps to remove traces of fluff. Unpicking dark thread from light fabric is rarely successful, as microscopic fibers remain in the holes and leave a dark shadow forevermore.

NEEDLE CASE

Color Key

	DMC/Anchor
✕✕	3755/140
....	Seam lines
——	Cutting line
☆	Middle point

NOTES

Use three strands of embroidery floss to work all the cross stitches.

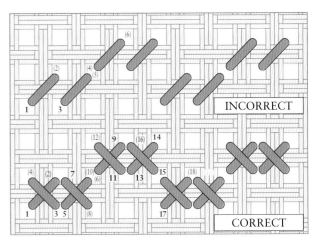

12 Work the required number of cross stitches to the end of the line, as indicated on the chart on page 27, counting your stitches and matching them to the squares on the chart.

13 *Row 2* Work the stitches in the order suggested in the lower portion of the diagram at right. The figures in parentheses indicate that the needle is to be inserted from the front of the work to the back. Frequently with full cross stitch a situation will arise where, in order to keep the bottom stitches lying in the same direction, a more complicated route has to be worked to ensure that existing stitches are not undone. The stitch between holes 5 and 6 is a good example. If it was worked in the same direction as the first two stitches, the stitch between 3 and 4 would be undone. The working order shown above is therefore recommended.

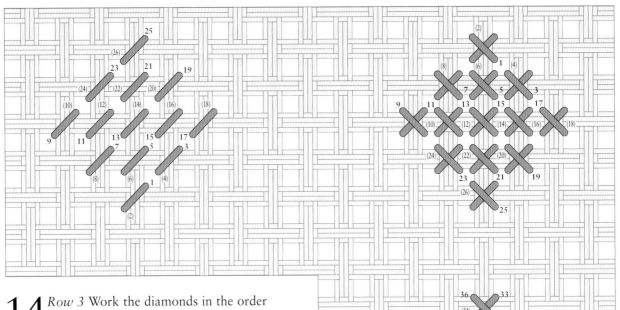

14 *Row 3* Work the diamonds in the order shown in the diagrams above and right to ensure that your crosses are correctly formed. Finish off the thread at the end of each diamond. Little tails and tufts on the back of the work will show through when the work is mounted and spoil its appearance. Providing the thread is properly secured, it is safe to cut the tail off very close to the work. More work is spoiled by failure to finish off neatly than by any other error.

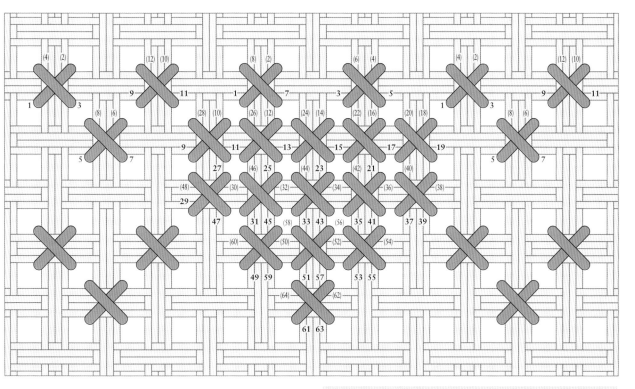

15 *Row 4* Work the solid hearts first in the order shown in the diagram above. Rejoin the thread to the back of a worked heart (p. 26), then work the top three linking cross stitches. Continue working in this way to the end of the row. Follow the same procedure to work the linking stitches at the bottom.

An Expert's Secret

Plan the route of your stitching very carefully. Always aim to run the thread away from a hole at an angle that forms a neat cross. Diagram A below shows a cross stitch correctly formed, where the thread has been taken from hole 4 in any of the directions shown by the arrows. Diagram B shows a cross stitch with an untidy long "leg" formed by taking the thread forward to the next hole. On occasion it may appear that more thread is used on the back of the work, but it is a false economy to sacrifice the appearance of the work for a few inches of thread.

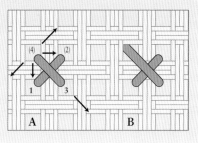

MAKING THE NEEDLE CASE (STEPS 16 – 22)

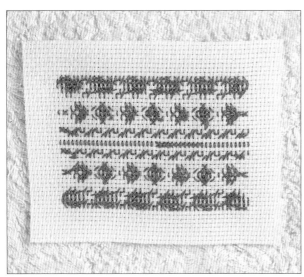

16 Remove the work from the hoop, then unpick and discard the basting threads. Trim the embroidered fabric (the front of the needle case) to the size shown on the chart. If necessary, press the finished work.

17 To press, lay a thick, fluffy, white terry towel on a flat surface (see Pressing Embroidery box opposite). Place your embroidery face down on the towel and cover it with a clean, white cotton cloth. Iron the work with a moderately hot iron.

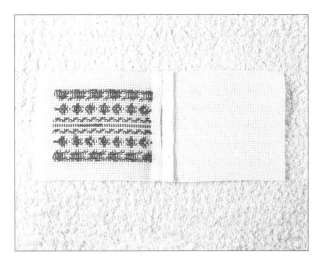

18 Cut the smaller piece of Aida (the back of the needle case) to the same size as the front. Place the two pieces of fabric right sides together and using sewing thread seam them together with a backstitch or a machine straight stitch, leaving a 2in (5cm) opening at the center of the seam. Press the seam open.

19 Place the embroidery and the cotton backing fabric right sides together and using sewing thread stitch around the seam line. Clip the corners and trim the seam allowance to ¼in (6mm) and turn right side out.

Pressing Embroidery

Sometimes it is necessary to iron finished work. Using a thick, fluffy, white terry towel allows the stitches to sink into the pile so that they are not flattened while the back of the work is pressed. Pressing stitches on a hard surface risks ruining them, making them flat and lifeless.

20 Use neat and tiny slip stitches to close the opening.

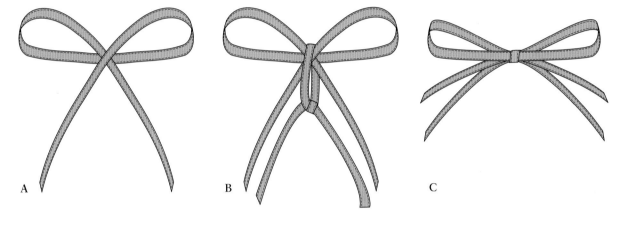

A   B   C

21 Trim the outer edges of the needle case with lace or braid. Add a small ribbon bow as the finishing touch. To make the bow, cut a length of ribbon and fold to form two loops as shown in

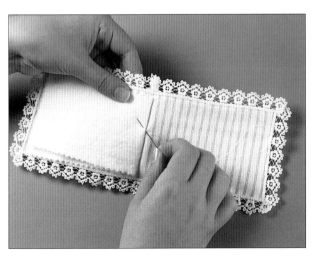

diagram A above. Cut another length of ribbon and knot it around the center as in diagram B above. Pull the knot tight, tease into shape and trim ends as in diagram C above.

22 Cut a piece of felt to hold the needles; for a decorative finish, cut the felt with pinking shears. Fold the needle case and the felt in half and stitch the felt to the inside of the needle case along the crease.

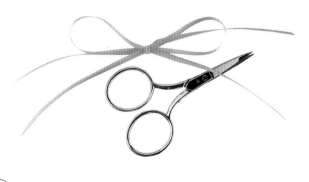

MULTICOLORED CROSS STITCH

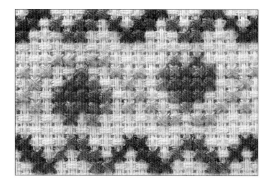

*T*here are hundreds of shades of embroidery floss
to choose from, and as you progress you will
acquire a wide selection of colors. The choice may
seem bewildering at first, but whether a pattern requires
only a few colors or a multitude, the harmonious use
of color is one of the great joys of cross stitch.

BOOKMARK
Finished Size: 7½ x 2in (19 x 5cm). Stitch Count: 83 x 20

Just five shades of embroidery floss have been used for this project, simplicity being the key. Two shades of pink, two of lavender, and a green are combined to make a pretty bookmark, giving you practice at changing colors in cross stitch. As an exercise in color selection, try working the pattern in different color combinations; you will soon discover what works and what does not.

When choosing colors for yourself, place the skeins on the fabric that you are going to use, as the background can affect the colors. If one or some of the colors are not harmonious they will stand out and beg to be changed. If you are very unsure of your ability to pick colors, make a note of color combinations that please you in other people's work, magazines, books, and so on, and use these colors in your own projects.

You Will Need
- *8in (20cm) embroidery hoop*
- *12 x 12in (30.5 x 30.5cm) waste fabric*
- *3 x 9in (7.5 x 23cm) 11-count Aida fabric, in cream*
- *Sewing thread*
- *Embroidery floss as in the color key*
- *Thread organizer*
- *Two tapestry needles, size 24*
- *3 x 9in (7.5 x 23cm) iron-on interfacing*
- *22in (56cm) length of cotton lace edging*
- *Short length of 1/8in (3mm) wide coordinating embroidery ribbon to make into a bow*

STORING THREAD ON AN ORGANIZER (STEPS 1 – 2)

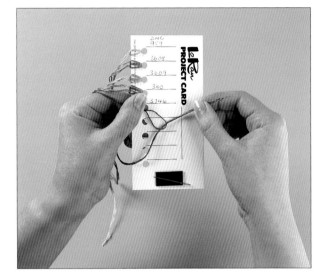

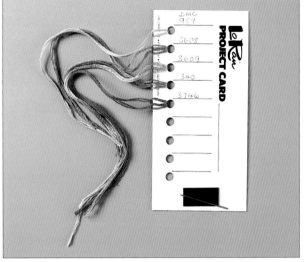

1 To prevent precious thread from getting lost or tangled into an irretrievable mess, mount spare strands onto a thread organizer. To do this, fold the strands in half to form a loop, pass the loop through the hole in the organizer and pass the ends of the strands through the loop.

2 Write the thread number next to the hole it occupies; this is particularly important when working with similar shades of one color. As you work, finish off each area of color as it is completed and store leftover thread on the organizer until it is needed again.

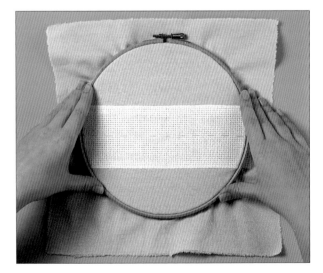

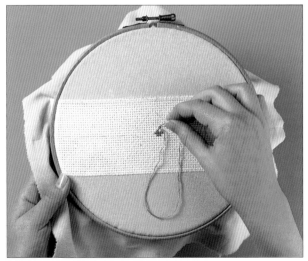

3 Stitch the strip of Aida embroidery fabric onto the waste fabric (p. 19) and then mount the waste fabric into the hoop (p. 17). Starting with the correct color (as indicated by the central square on the chart), thread the needle (p. 19).

4 Using a knotless start (p. 24), begin stitching the heart at the center of the design using the color indicated on the chart. Follow the guidelines for working cross stitch described in Skill 1. (Refer also to The Golden Rules of Cross Stitch on p. 117.)

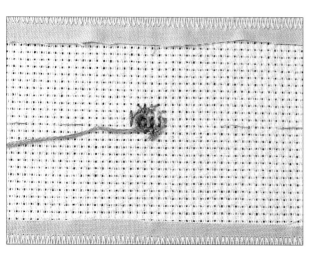

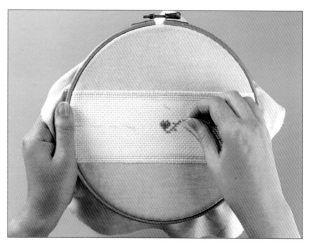

5 When one area of color is complete, join in another color using the technique for adding a new thread (p. 26).

6 When the central heart is complete, work the whole of the green vine—this establishes the positions of the rest of the hearts, which can now be worked without complicated counting across bare fabric.

An Expert's Secret

As you work, twists will develop on your thread and if they are not removed the thread will twist tighter and tighter. This will not give good coverage of the fabric. To prevent this, allow the needle to dangle from the work regularly so it untwists, or turn the needle in your hand as you work to remove any twists.

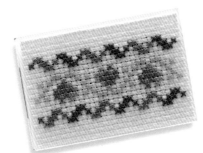

7 For the lavender border, thread one tapestry needle with light lavender and one with dark lavender. Work the first repeat with one needle and the second repeat with the other. On the back of the work, thread the first needle through the back of the stitches on the second repeat and bring the thread to the surface ready to work the third repeat. (You can bring thread from one area to another on the back of the work without finishing off and starting again only if it can be threaded through the back of existing stitches without showing on the surface.)

Make a magnetic note holder from the same design (see chart, p. 36). Stitch on 11-count cream Aida and cover the back with iron-on interfacing. Cut the work to size and slip it into the mount. Some all-purpose adhesive on the back of the inside of the mount will prevent the work from slipping.

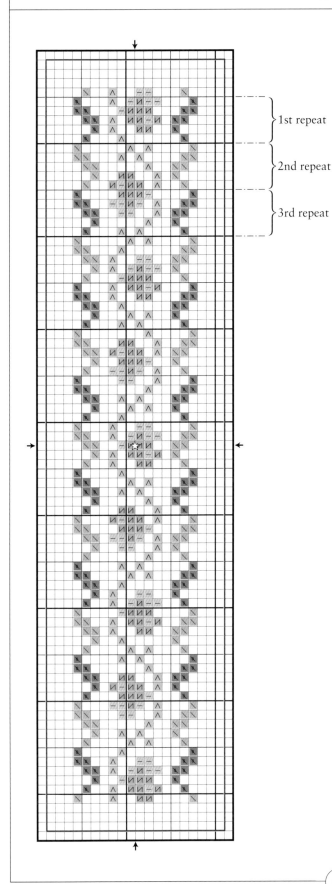

1st repeat

2nd repeat

3rd repeat

MAKING THE BOOKMARK
(STEPS 8 – 10)

8 When the embroidery is finished, remove the fabric from the hoop, cut away and discard the waste fabric (p. 19) and remove the basting threads from the embroidery. To stiffen the bookmark and hide the back of the work, back it with iron-on interfacing. Lay a white, fluffy, terry towel on a flat surface and put the embroidery face down onto it. Lay the iron-on interfacing over the back of the embroidery. Then following the manufacturer's instructions on the interfacing, press the work with an iron until it has bonded with the embroidery.

BOOKMARK
Color Key

	DMC/Anchor
;	Cross stitch
⁒⁒	3609/85
ⵜⵜ	3746/118
◥◥	340/117
ИИ	3608/86
ΛΛ	959/186

— Cutting line

☆ Middle point

NOTES

Use three strands of embroidery floss to work all cross stitches.

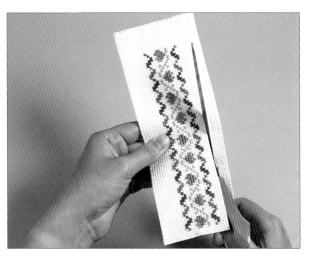

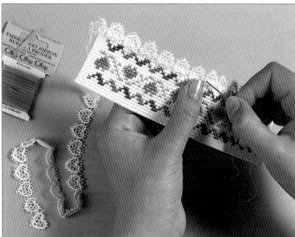

9 Using dressmaking scissors, cut the backed embroidery along the cutting line marked on the chart. Carefully oversew the edges with a machine zigzag stitch or overcast neatly by hand.

10 Stitch a pretty cotton lace edging around the edges—here hearts have been chosen to mirror the hearts in the design. Trim with a ribbon bow (see Skill 1, Step 21, p. 31). Using embroidery ribbon to form a flat bow will not distort the pages of a book.

TOWEL

To perk up a plain towel, a section of the bookmark design has been stitched and the colors changed to complement the towel. (See p. 32 for advice on choosing your own colors.) Following the chart on page 113, stitch the design on 1in (2.5cm) wide white, scalloped-edged Aida band. Stitch enough repeats of the design to fit the towel width, plus ½in (1.25cm) each end. Stitch the band to the towel, turning the ends in neatly on the back of the towel.

BACKSTITCH LETTERING

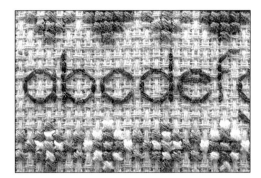

ackstitch is so called because all the stitches worked on the front surface of the fabric are worked in a backward direction, while those on the back of the work go forward. This ensures that the slight backward pull on each stitch gives it definition and neatness. Backstitch lettering is a useful addition to your cross stitch as it will allow you to work texts and personalize any work with names and dates. Finished pieces of work are more interesting if signed and dated. On larger pieces of stitching include the date of commencement as well as the date of completion to make sure that future generations will appreciate your effort. When working backstitch for lettering to personalize a piece, you will generally need to use two strands of embroidery floss in the needle.

A FIRST SAMPLER

Finished Size: 3 x 4¼in (7.5 x 11cm). Stitch Count: 59 x 39

During the eighteenth and nineteenth centuries, cross stitch samplers were worked by school-children as a classroom exercise. They provided a method of teaching the skills of needlework and also literacy, as alphabets were generally included in the design. Some of the other traditional motifs commonly worked were houses, trees, animals, flowers, and hearts. These elements are combined here to produce your first cross stitch sampler on a finer fabric and in colors that echo the soft tones of antique samplers. Also incorporated are letters and numbers worked in backstitch to give you practice in backstitch lettering.

You Will Need
- *7in (18cm) embroidery hoop*
- *11 x 11in (28 x 28cm) 14-count Rustico Aida fabric*
- *Embroidery floss as in the color key*
- *Two tapestry needles, size 26*
- *Frame with a 3¼ x 4½in (8 x 11.5cm) opening*

A First Sampler

Color Key

DMC/Anchor
Cross stitch

• •	781/309
v v	Ecru/926
◻ ◻	927/849
– –	3768/779
+ +	502/876
× ×	833/907
= =	3041/871
∷ ∷	356/1013

Backstitch

—— 924/851

—— 919/340

☆   Middle point

NOTES

Use two strands of embroidery floss to work all cross stitches. Work backstitches with two strands.

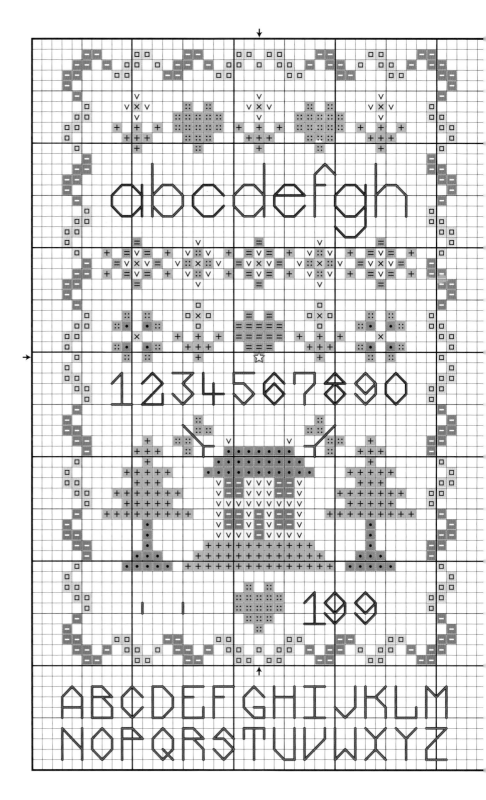

1 Prepare the fabric for work (p. 16) and mount it into the embroidery hoop (p. 17).

LOOP STARTING METHOD
(STEPS 2 – 5)
This method can be used to start a thread neatly whenever you are using an even number of strands.

2 Cut a 20in (51cm) length of embroidery floss and separate one strand from the length. Double it to give two strands. Thread the two ends through the eye of the needle to form a loop that hangs from the needle.

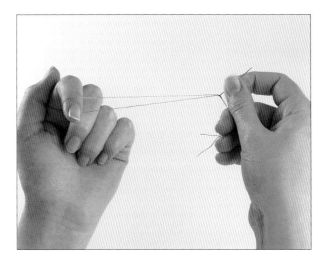

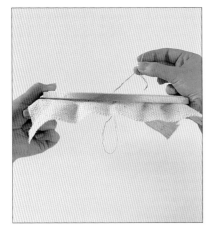

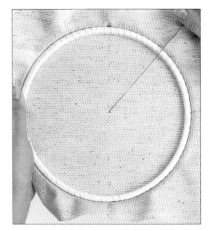

3 Bring the needle to the surface of the fabric at the starting point, leaving the loop on the back of the work.

4 Take the needle to the back of the work to make the first half of the cross stitch and thread the needle through the loop.

5 Tighten the thread and you have a neat, knotless start.

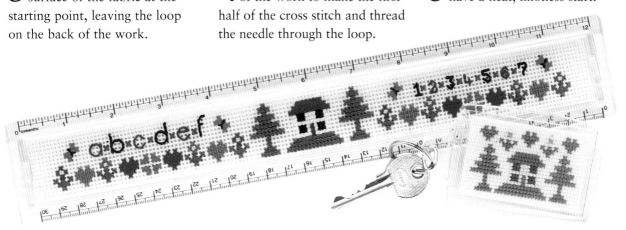

Adapting designs is easy and addictive. See Exploring the Options (p. 108) for charts, instructions, and ideas.

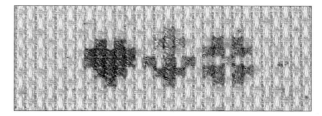

6 Now start your cross stitching by first working the heart in the center of the design, following the guidelines for working cross stitch described in Skill 1. (Refer also to The Golden Rules of Cross Stitch on p. 117.)

7 When one area of color is complete, join in another thread color (p. 26) and continue to build up the design. Finish off each area of color as it is completed and store leftover thread on an organizer until it is needed again (p. 34).

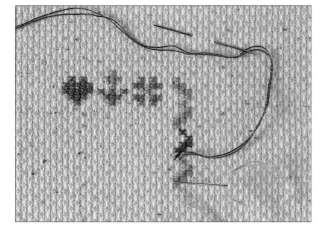

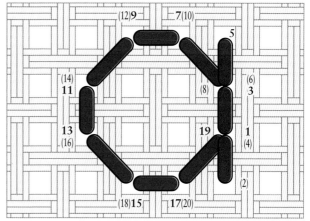

8 When stitching the border, work with two needles, one threaded with light blue and one with darker blue. Alternate colors can be threaded through the back of the stitches ready to work the next repeat, but care should be taken not to distort existing stitches.

9 To work the letter "a," use the loop starting method (see previous page). Then, closely following the diagram above, bring the needle out at 1 and in at (2), out at 3 and in at (4), out at 5 and in at (6), out at 7 and in at (8), out at 9 and in at (10), and so on.

10 Continue in this way all around the letter "a," ensuring that all the stitches on the surface of the fabric are worked in a backward direction. Finish the thread off neatly by weaving into the back of a few stitches on the reverse side. Work the letter "b" in the same way, planning your route around the letter to ensure the backward pull on each stitch, as shown in the diagram right. For each letter and number, start your backstitching at point 1 each time, taking your needle down at (2), up at 3, down at (4), and so on.

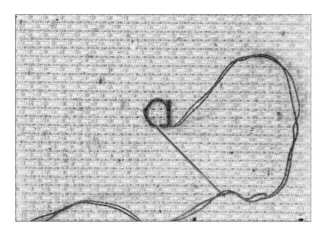

An Expert's Secret

Do not be tempted to carry your thread from the "a" to the "c" across the back of the work. Each stitched area of a design should be finished off neatly before moving on to the next. Thread must never be jumped across the back of bare fabric, as a ghostly trail will show through and spoil the appearance of the work. However, threads can be worked through the back of worked stitches, as in the border (see Step 8). But when working the trees, for example, finish each off and do not jump down to stitch the grass.

11 When the letters and numbers are complete, use the alphabet and numbers provided on the chart (and the photograph of the finished sampler as an example) to stitch your initials and the year in the space provided. Remember to align the initials with the date. Finally, work the bodies and antennae of the two butterflies in backstitch.

12 When the embroidery is complete, take it out of the hoop and remove the basting threads. If necessary, press the embroidery (Step 17, p. 30). Frame your finished work in the frame of your choice to preserve it for posterity. (See p. 110 for framing tips.)

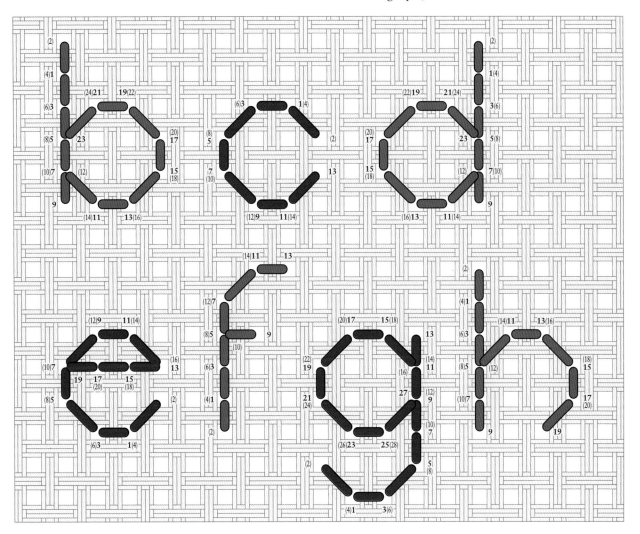

BACKSTITCH OUTLINING

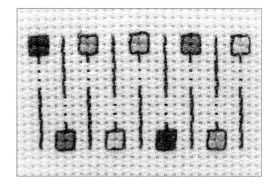

*N*ot only is backstitch used alongside cross stitch to form lettering, it is also used to outline and add detail and definition to your work. Outlining gives the cross stitch a straight edge and a finished look, and is worked after the cross stitch has been completed. Usually fewer strands of floss are used for outlining than for the cross stitch it complements.

CHATELAINE

Finished Size: Chatelaine 1 x 46in (2.5 x 117cm); Pincushion 3 x 4in (7.5 x 10cm)
Stitch Count: Chatelaine 10 x 703; Pincushion 13 x 26

Now you are ready to progress to working on Aida band, a finer fabric than you have used before. What better way to learn the skill of backstitch outlining than by making another stitcher's aid? No more lost needles and scissors; a chatelaine, to hang around your neck, will keep your pincushion and embroidery scissors always to hand.

If you are pressed for time, consider working just a few of the designs at each end of the band, enough to feel that you have mastered the technique.

You Will Need
- *Small embroidery frame (optional)*
- *50in (127cm) scalloped-edge 14-count Aida band, 1in (2.5cm) wide, in white with sky blue edges*
- *Embroidery floss as listed in the color key*
- *Tapestry needle, size 26*
- *50in (127cm) length of ⅝in (15mm) wide satin ribbon, in white*
- *White sewing thread*
- *7in (18cm) scalloped-edge 14-count Aida band, 4in (10cm) wide, in white with sky blue edges*
- *Small flexi-hoop*
- *Washable stuffing*
- *Sharp-pointed embroidery scissors*

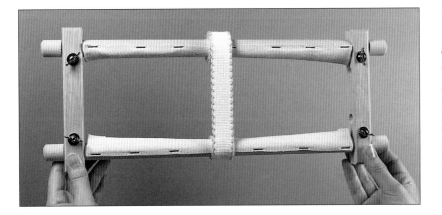

1 Fold the long Aida band in half lengthwise to find the center and mark with basting thread (p. 16). Mount the band onto a small embroidery frame (p. 18), but do not lace the sides. If you prefer to do so, it is quite acceptable to work Aida bands in the hand without a frame.

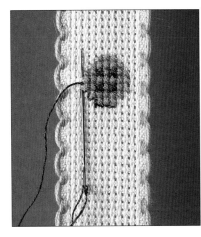

2 Start by working the tape-measure design (A) in the middle of the band. Work the threads and pins design (B) twice, one on each side of design A, then stitch the threads and buttons design (C) on each end of the band, leaving ten blocks or squares of fabric unworked between each design. Work each design in cross stitch before outlining it. Start the backstitch outlining with one of the buttons as follows. First, thread your needle with one strand of floss and join the thread to the back of the cross stitches (p. 26).

3 Work the outline of the button, making backstitches in the order shown in the diagram above. Bring your needle out at 1 and in at (2), out at 3 and in at (4), out at 5 and in at (6), out at 7 and in at (8), out at 9 and in at (10), out at 11 and in at (12), out at 13 and in at

(14), out at 15 and in at (16), out at 17 and in at (18). Continue this sequence all round the button, ending by putting your needle in at (56). To complete the button, work the two central backstitches over the top of the center cross stitch as shown above.

CHATELAINE

Color Key

	DMC/Anchor Cross stitch
– –	413/236
I I	744/301
1 1	Blanc/1
2 2	605/50
3 3	799/136
4 4	762/234
5 5	729/890
6 6	993/186
II II	800/144

	Backstitch
▬	413/236
—	Edge of ribbon
☆	Middle point

NOTES

Use two strands of embroidery floss to work all cross stitches. Work backstitches with one strand.

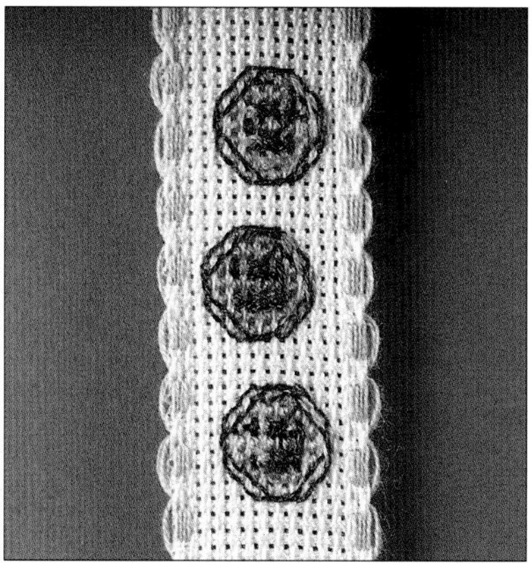

4 Remember that all stitches on the surface of the work are made in a backward direction, and all stitches on the back of the work should go forward. The photograph above shows the back of three buttons when the backstitch outlining has been completed.

A

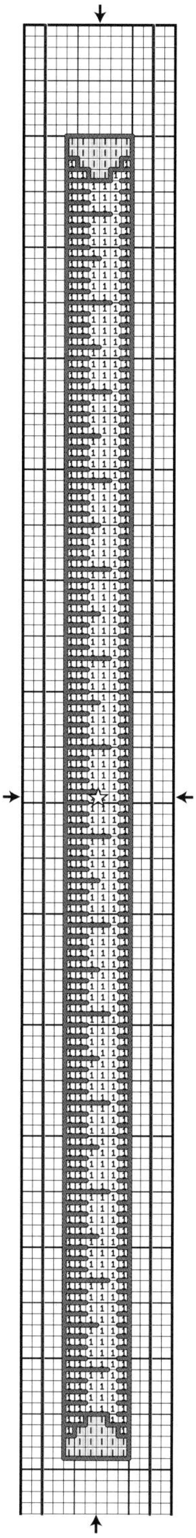

B

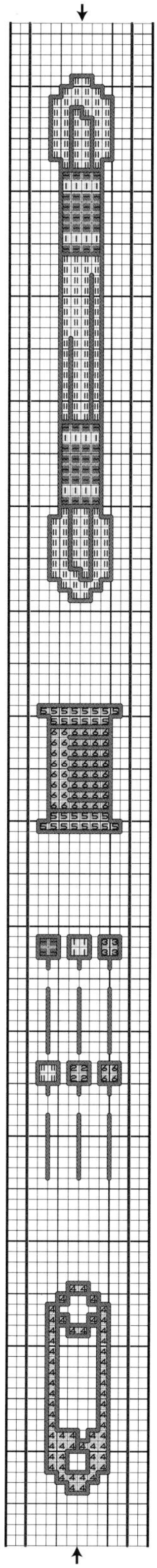

C

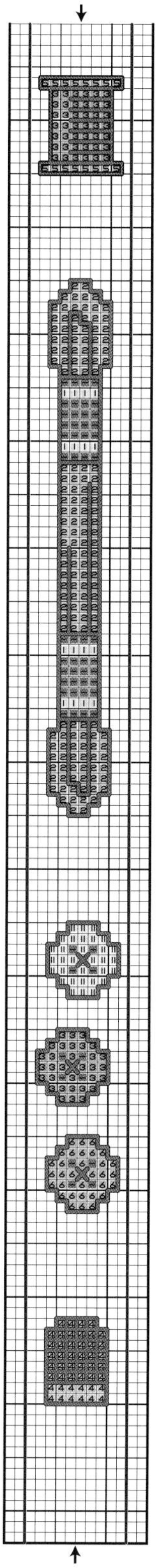

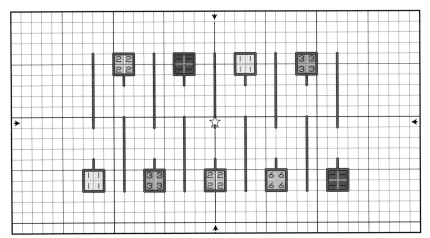

PINCUSHION

Color Key

DMC/Anchor

Cross stitch	Backstitch
▬ 413/236	—— 413/236
2 2 605/50	
3 3 799/136	☆ Middle point
6 6 993/186	
I I I 744/301	

NOTES

Use two strands of embroidery floss to work all cross stitches. Work backstitches with one strand.

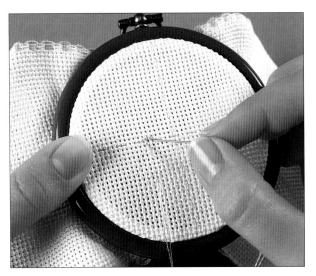

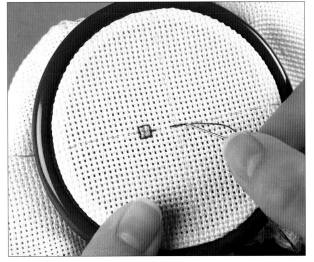

5 Now work the pincushion. Prepare the short Aida band, mark the center with basting thread (p. 17) and mount it into a small flexi-hoop (p. 18). Following the chart, work the design of pins.

6 Using the chart to guide you, add black backstitched pin lengths to the completed cross stitch.

An Expert's Secret

Do not take short cuts when outlining in backstitch. The temptation can be to work holes as follows: out at 1 and in at 2, out at 1 and in at 3, out at 4 and in at 3, out at 4 and in at 5, and so on. You may appear to be saving thread by adopting this method, but you are not back stitching and every other stitch will be a long one.

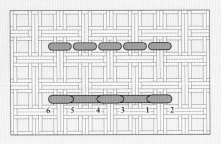

MAKING THE PINCUSHION (STEPS 7 – 8)

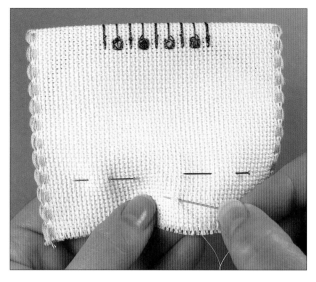

7 Remove basting threads and press the work (Step 17, p. 30). Fold the fabric right sides together. Stitch the back seam, allowing ⅜in (1cm) seam allowance. Turn right side out.

8 With wrong sides together, stitch the bottom seam and stuff the pincushion lightly with washable stuffing. Stitch the top seam, leaving a 1in (2.5cm) opening in the center.

MAKING THE CHATELAINE (STEPS 9 – 11)

9 Remove the stitched chatelaine band from the frame, if used, and remove the basting threads. If necessary press the work (Step 17, p. 30).

10 Hand stitch the white satin ribbon to the wrong side of the embroidery so that it neatly covers the back of the work.

11 Neaten the ends of the band. Fold one end of the band through one finger hole of the scissors and stitch it in place on the back. Slip the other end into the opening in the seam of the pincushion and slipstitch the gap closed.

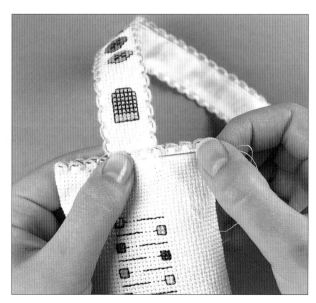

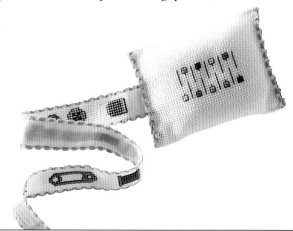

FRENCH KNOTS

The French knot is a valuable addition to cross stitch designs. Once mastered, it can be added to form eyes on faces, worked in groups to make flowers, or for many other small but important details. When I first started stitching people onto samplers and greeting cards I had to master French knots very quickly. I used them for eyes, and many of my characters ended up with squints until I perfected the art of the perfectly round French knot. There is widespread belief that they are difficult to work, but in fact they are simplicity itself if a few basic rules are observed.

✗ ✗ ✗ ✗

LAVENDER SACHET BAG

Finished Size: 2½ x 2½ in (6.5 x 6.5cm). Stitch Count: 45 x 45

To banish forever the myth that French knots are to be dreaded, work this lavender sachet bag, which gives you more than 100 French knots on which to practice. They are grouped so closely together in the spikes of lavender that if the odd one goes awry it will not show, and by the end of the pattern you will wonder what the fuss was about.

If you want a pretty piece of work like this to be on show permanently, and not hidden away in a drawer or wardrobe, consider framing it (see p. 54).

You Will Need
- *4in (10cm) embroidery hoop*
- *8 x 8in (20 x 20cm) 14-count Aida fabric, in cream*
- *Embroidery floss as in the color key*
- *Tapestry needle, size 26 for cross stitch*
- *Tapestry needle, size 24 for French knots*
- *6 x 6in (15 x 15cm) cotton backing fabric in a complementary color*
- *White sewing cotton*
- *Dried lavender or potpourri*
- *21in (53.5cm) lace or braid*
- *Scraps of ¹⁄₁₆ in (1.5mm) wide ribbon in a complementary color*
- *Trimmings of your choice*

LAVENDER SACHET BAG

Color Key:

DMC/Anchor

Cross stitch		French knot	
⊓⊓	993/186	◉	3746/1030
▓▓	3746/1030	◈	341/117
⏐⏐	341/117	◉	340/118
⏐⏐	340/118	☆	Middle point

NOTES

Use two strands of embroidery floss to work all cross stitches. Work French knots with two strands.

1 Using the loop starting method (p. 41), work all cross stitches first, using the size 26 tapestry needle. Bring your size 24 needle out ready to work the bottom French knot on the left-hand spike of lavender.

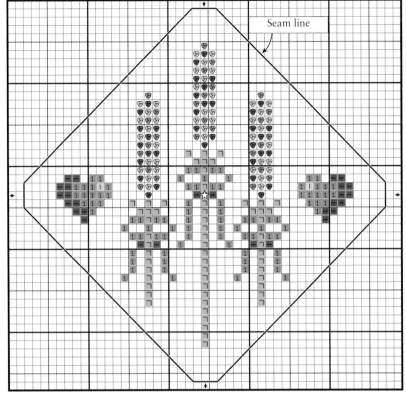

Seam line

2 Bring the needle out in the middle of the block, one pair of threads to the right of where you want the French knot to lie. Lay the hoop on a table or your knee so that both hands are free.

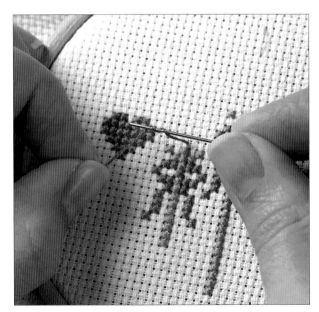

3 Holding the thread between finger and thumb in your left hand and the needle in your right, twist the thread twice around the needle in a counterclockwise direction.

4 Insert the needle back into the fabric, one pair of threads to the left. Gently tighten, but not overtighten, the twists around the needle.

5 Lift the hoop in your left hand, holding the thread coming from the needle firmly against the fabric. Very gently and slowly pull the needle through to the back without allowing the twists to unravel.

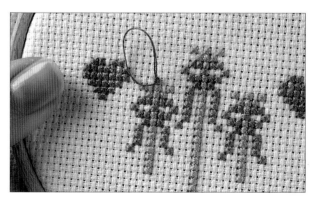

6 Pull the last 1in (2.5cm) of thread through extra carefully to form the French knot.

An Expert's Secret

When working a French knot on an Aida block, always work over the central threads. Close examination of Aida blocks will show that half of the blocks have central threads that lie horizontally, and half of the blocks have central threads that lie vertically. If the block has vertical center threads, bring the needle out on the right of the threads and go back in to the left of them so that the central threads support the knot and prevent it from sinking to the back of the fabric. If the block has horizontal center threads, bring the needle out above the threads and go back in below them for the same reason. You may wish to turn the fabric in your hand when working in this direction. The secret of success is to pull the thread through very gently, as any tugging will tighten the twists so that the eye of the needle is unable to pass through them, and any sudden jerk will pull the knot through to the back of the work. Do not be tempted to work French knots with more than two twists. If a bigger knot is required, use more strands of floss or a thicker needle. If more twists are used the knot will be distorted and not circular.

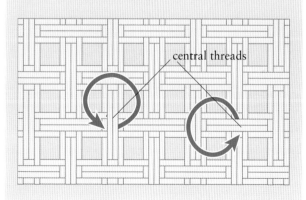

central threads

7 Finish all the dark-colored French knots, then change to the lighter thread color and continue making knots on the left-hand lavender spike. Next, work the lighest knots. When they are complete, work the right-hand spike, leaving your practiced and best efforts for the central spike.

Rather than have your lavender design out of sight most of the time, you could frame it (see p. 110).

MAKING THE LAVENDER SACHET BAG (STEPS 8 – 9)

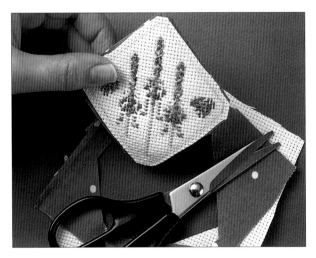

8 Remove the embroidery from the hoop and remove all basting threads. If necessary press the work (Step 17, p. 30). Place the backing fabric over the embroidery, right sides together. Sew around the seam line with sewing thread, leaving a 1in (2.5cm) opening on one side. Trim the fabric to ¼in (5mm) from the seam line and clip corners.

9 Turn right side out. Fill the sachet with dried lavender or potpourri and slipstitch the opening closed. Trim the edge of the sachet with lace or braid. Make a hanging loop and decorative bow from ribbon and trim the corners of the sachet with whatever trimmings take your fancy.

WORKING WITH PLASTIC CANVAS

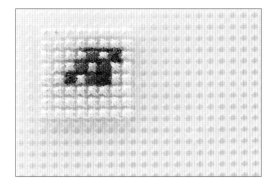

*P*lastic canvas makes it possible to work three-dimensional projects in cross stitch. A relatively recent innovation, plastic canvas is made of a rigid but flexible material that can be cut into any shape, will not fray, and can be assembled into a wide variety of formed objects. It is readily available in a number of counts and preformed shapes (see photographs on p. 12) with holes spaced at regular intervals to form a mesh. Stitches are worked over intersections of the mesh, which cannot distort; therefore, it is not necessary to use an embroidery hoop or frame when working on plastic canvas.

PINCUSHION BASKET

Finished Size (including handle): 3 x 2 x 3in (7.5 x 5 x 7.5cm)
Stitch Counts: Side 42 x 22, End 26 x 22, Base 42 x 26, Handle 58 x 7

A decorative pincushion basket that uses simple rectangular shapes has been designed as your introduction to working with plastic canvas. The pincushion is removable and the basket can hold any small gift that you please. For example, at Easter it could be filled with tiny Easter eggs or with little candies at Christmas.

You Will Need
- *One sheet 14-count plastic canvas at least 6½in x 5in (16.5 x 13 cm)*
- *Embroidery floss as in the color key*
- *Tapestry needle, size 26*
- *General household scissors*
- *4 x 8in (10 x 20cm) white felt*
- *Clear, all-purpose glue*
- *24in (61cm) length of ⅛in (3mm) wide ribbon, in lavender*
- *6 x 5in (15 x 13cm)*

coordinating cotton fabric
- *White sewing thread*
- *Small amount of stuffing*
- *Decorative pearlized pins*

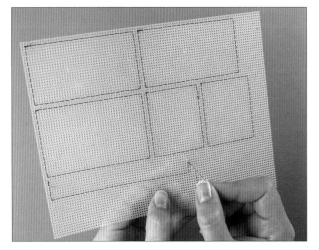

1 Baste the cutting lines shown on the chart to mark out the six pieces that make up the basket onto your sheet of plastic canvas. You should end up with two long sides, two ends, one base, and one handle.

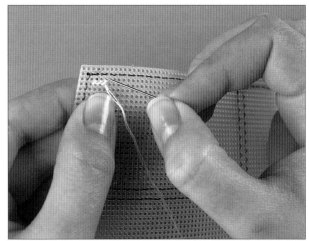

2 Hold the plastic canvas in your hand and cross stitch exactly as if you were working on fabric. Starting with one of the long sides, and using the loop starting method (p. 41), begin by stitching one space in from the cutting line.

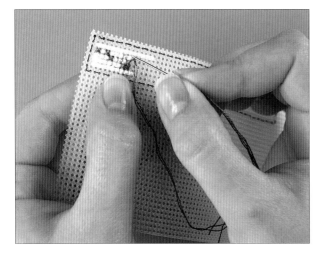

3 Following the chart on page 58, and making the color changes as necessary, complete the cross stitching on all six cut-out pieces of plastic canvas.

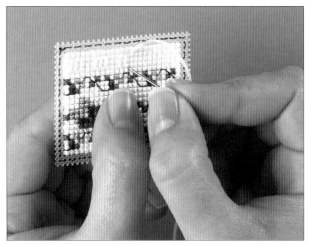

4 Work the vertical stitches that carry the ribbon using three strands of floss, in the positions marked on the chart.

An Expert's Secret

Experts would not dream of cheating by not stitching the base of the basket because it is rarely, if ever, on view... would they?

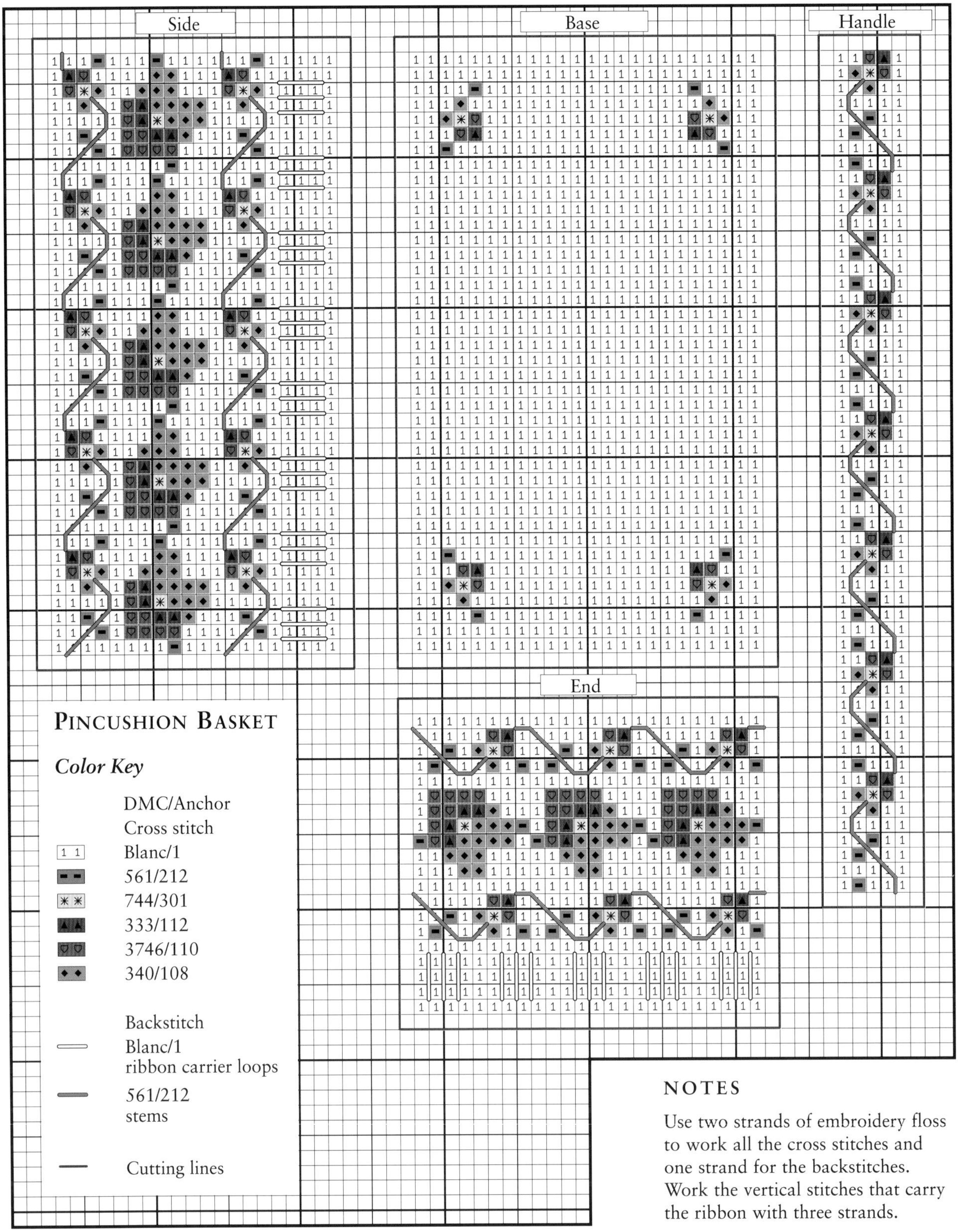

Side

Base

Handle

End

PINCUSHION BASKET

Color Key

DMC/Anchor
Cross stitch

`1 1`	Blanc/1
■ ■	561/212
✳ ✳	744/301
▲ ▲	333/112
♡ ♡	3746/110
◆ ◆	340/108

Backstitch

Blanc/1
ribbon carrier loops

561/212
stems

Cutting lines

NOTES

Use two strands of embroidery floss
to work all the cross stitches and
one strand for the backstitches.
Work the vertical stitches that carry
the ribbon with three strands.

MAKING THE BASKET (STEPS 5 – 12)

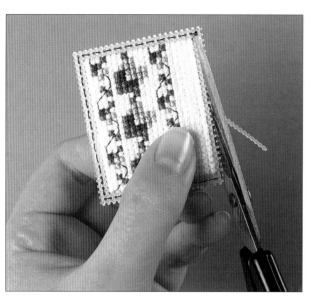

5 When the embroidery is complete, trim each piece of the basket along the cutting lines. Do not use sharp embroidery scissors for this as you will blunt them.

6 Aim for a straight edge on the plastic canvas and remove any indentations.

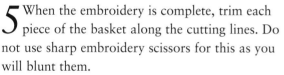

7 To line the basket, cut a piece of felt to fit each piece of the basket. Use the pieces as a cutting guide and then trim each piece of felt so that it is marginally smaller than the piece of plastic canvas it is going to line. Put the felt to one side.

This pretty basket can do more than house a pin-cushion. Filled with sweet things it makes an ideal gift, or it could be used as an Easter decoration.

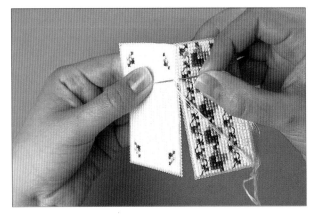

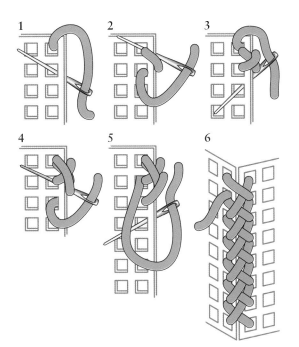

8 Join each of the long sides in turn to the base using the joining stitch shown right. This will give a decorative, braided finish. Now join the short ends to the base to form a basket, again using the joining stitch. Finally, using the same stitch, join the corners from the base upward.

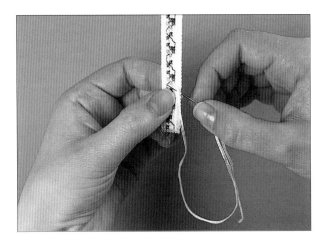

9 Work the edging stitch shown in the diagram below all round the top of the basket and down each side of the handle.

10 Line the handle by gluing the appropriate piece of felt in place on the back of the work. Stitch the ends of the handle to the sides of the basket on the inside.

11 Line the basket by gluing the other pieces of felt in their correct positions on the inside, so that the back of the work is covered.

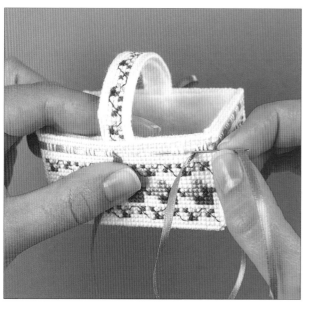

12 Cut the ribbon in half and, using the needle, thread one half at a time through the vertical carrying stitches so that the ends of the ribbon come out halfway around each side under the handle. Tie a bow on each side and trim the ends of the ribbon.

MAKING THE PINCUSHION (STEPS 13 – 15)

13 Using sewing thread, take fine running stitches around the edges of the piece of coordinating cotton fabric.

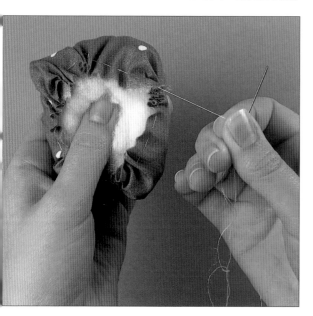

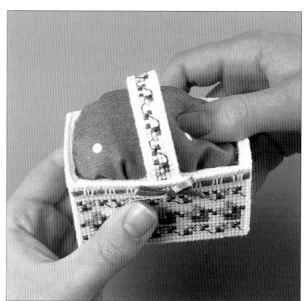

14 Place a small amount of stuffing in the center of the fabric, pull the running thread up around it to gather, forming a soft but compact pillow, and then tie off the thread securely.

15 Push the pillow into the basket so that the raw and gathered edges of the fabric are hidden. Finally, place the decorative pearlized pins in the pincushion, ready for use.

WORKING WITH PERFORATED PAPER

Perforated paper, sometimes known as stitching paper, enjoyed great popularity during the Victorian era. The vogue was to use the paper to stitch all manner of small items— bookmarks, needle cases, alphabets, as well as larger mottoes to frame and hang on the wall. In spite of its apparent fragility it is quite durable, allowing the edges to be cut into any shape without fraying. The revival of interest in Victorian crafts means that supplies are now available again. It can be bought in many colors, including gold and silver, and has a count of 14 holes to 1in (2.5cm).

✕ ✕ ✕ ✕

TREASURE BOX

Finished Size: 1 x 2 x 2in (2.5 x 5 x 5cm). Stitch Count: 72 x 72

The ability to cut and manipulate perforated paper is exploited to the full in this project. Here a simple pattern is cut and folded into a treasure box, something that would be impossible to do if the design were stitched on fabric or plastic canvas. Use the box to hold a favorite piece of jewelery, a sentimental memento, or any small treasure. Alternatively, treat a friend to a gift box that conceals a special birthday surprise.

You Will Need

- *One sheet of perforated paper, in off-white*
- *Steel ruler*
- *Lead pencil*
- *Embroidery floss as in the color key*
- *Tapestry needle, size 26*
- *Sharp paper-cutting scissors*
- *Craft knife*
- *Clear, all-purpose glue*
- *Paper clips*

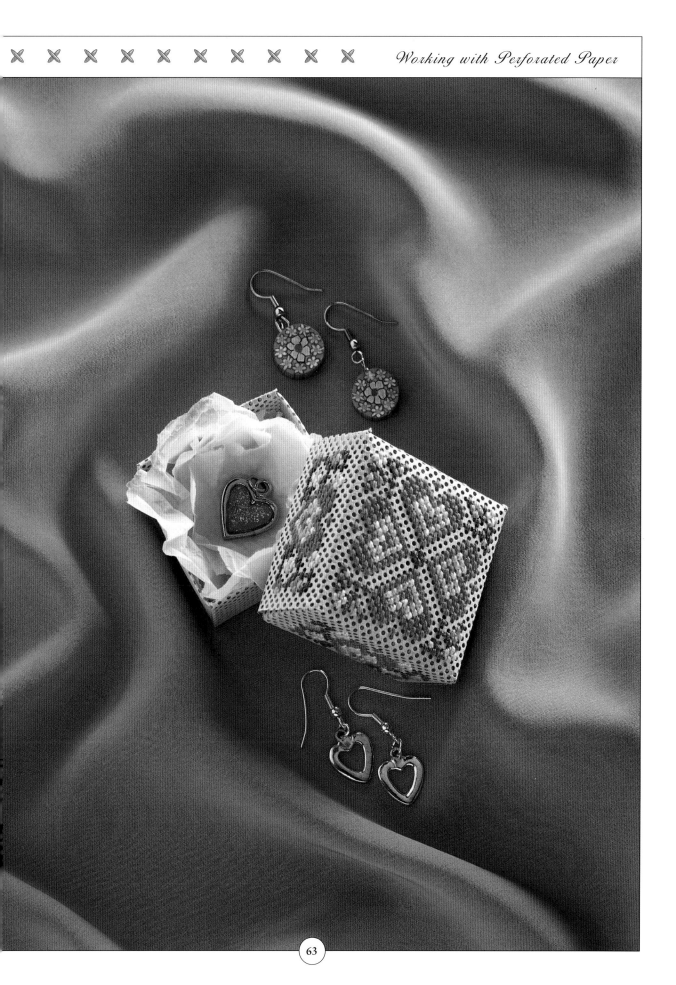

1 Using the chart to guide you, mark the outline of the embroidered lid (opposite) and the unworked base of the box (below) on the wrong side of the perforated paper using a pencil and ruler. (The rougher side of the paper is the wrong side.) First, mark the outermost square, then the diagonal lines within. (Stitches are worked over the solid areas of paper between holes, so your pencil marks need to run along lines of holes.)

2 Using the penciled lines on the back of the work as a guide, begin, with a knotless start (p. 24), to stitch in the center of the central diamond. Stitch the whole design, taking care not to form bulky lumps when you finish and start. (The smoother the work, the easier it will be to fold into an undistorted lid.) Plan your stitching route with great care, avoiding thread across the back of empty holes, where it will be visible.

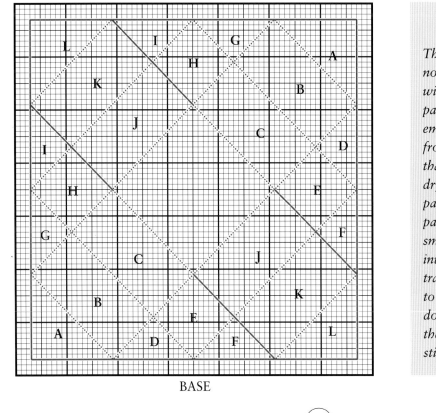

BASE

An Expert's Secret

The use of a hoop or frame is not necessary when working with perforated paper, but if the paper is mounted into an embroidery frame it suffers less from handling. Always ensure that your hands are clean and dry before handling perforated paper; hand cream can stain the paper and render it useless. Any small tears can be repaired invisibly on the back with transparent tape. Apply the tape to the torn area, smooth it down over the tear to restore the surface, and continue stitching through the tape.

LID

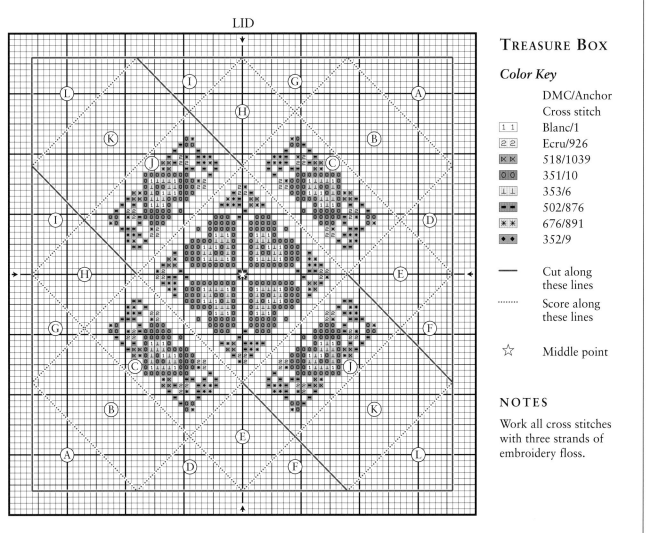

TREASURE BOX

Color Key

	DMC/Anchor Cross stitch
1 1	Blanc/1
2 2	Ecru/926
✕ ✕	518/1039
0 0	351/10
⊥ ⊥	353/6
▬ ▬	502/876
✳ ✳	676/891
◆ ◆	352/9

— Cut along these lines

...... Score along these lines

☆ Middle point

NOTES

Work all cross stitches with three strands of embroidery floss.

3 When the embroidery is complete, use sharp paper-cutting scissors to cut along the cutting lines of the embroidered lid. Make the four diagonal cuts marked on the chart.

4 Placing your work face down on a cutting mat, score along the rest of the diagonal fold lines on the back, using a craft knife held against a steel ruler. Score lightly to avoid cutting right through the paper.

FOLDING THE LID AND BASE (STEPS 5 – 11)

5 With the wrong side of the work facing you, fold AB over C.

6 Stand BC upright to form one side of the box. Repeat the sequence on the other side.

VALENTINE CARD

This pretty Valentine card has been created by using different components of the treasure box design and a different color scheme (see p. 116 for chart). Stitch it on white 14-count Aida to fit a ready-made card with a 3¼in (8cm)-square opening. Mount the work into the card mat (p. 88) and trim by gluing on pearl beading, rickrack, lace, or other trimmings of your choice. For other ideas on adapting the treasure box design to decorate a coaster, a spectacle case, or a flexi-hoop picture, see Exploring the Options, page 108.

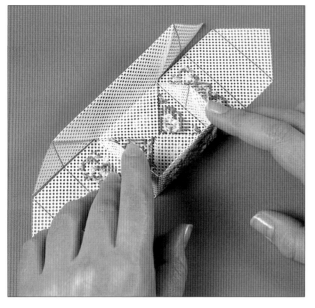

7 Fold DEF inward at right angles to AB. Fold GHI inward at right angles to AB.

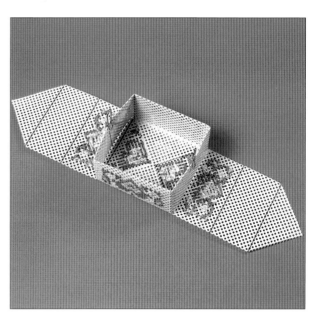

8 Turn the box around and repeat Step 7 on the other side. Overlap DEF and GHI, lining them up carefully. Use a dab of glue to stick them together and hold until dry with a paper clip. Repeat on the other side.

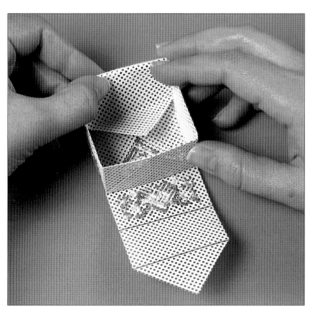

9 Lift J up to cover the outside of DEFGHI. Fold K over to the inside of DEFGHI and press L down into the base of the box. Repeat on the other side.

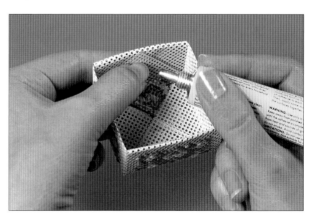

10 Lift both flaps marked L and both flaps marked A, and place a small dab of glue underneath them to hold them in place. The lid is now folded, and the perforated paper forms a lining to hide the back of your stitching.

11 To complete the box, repeat Steps 3–10 with the base of the box (which has no embroidery), then place the base inside the lid.

WORKING WITH AIDA PLUS

*A*ida Plus is a modern fabric that has many of the useful properties of perforated paper and none of its weaknesses. You can cut it, trim it, and shape it without any unraveling, fraying, or splitting, and, unlike perforated paper, it is hand washable and will not tear. As this project demonstrates, it even allows you to weave with

it. This would be difficult with other fabrics, which would fray, or with perforated paper, which might tear. Aida Plus is 14-count and available in 9 x 12in (23 x 30.5cm) sheets, in a variety of colors. The fabric has a treated backing that prevents distortion, so no hoop or frame is necessary.

CHRISTMAS HEART-SHAPED BASKETS
Finished Size: 3½ x 3½in (9 x 9cm). Stitch Count: 96 x 33

Deck your Christmas tree with cross stitched baskets filled with sweets or other goodies. A basket can be stitched in an evening, and the weaving takes only a few minutes. For variety, you could try combining different colors of Aida Plus, for example, green with red or red with white. Pink with white, or pale blue with white with complementary cross stitch and frothy lace trimmings would make a lovely gift for another occasion.

You Will Need
- *One sheet 14-count Aida Plus fabric, in emerald green*
- *One sheet 14-count Aida Plus fabric, in white or red*
- *Embroidery floss as in the color key*
- *Tapestry needle, size 26*
- *Sharp, fine-pointed scissors*
- *Scraps of braid, lace, ribbon, and cord*
- *Clear, all-purpose glue*

NAPKIN HOLDER
This napkin holder uses the motifs from the main project. Work on white perforated paper (chart, p. 114), back with pretty wrapping paper, cut to size, and place in the mount.

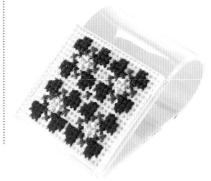

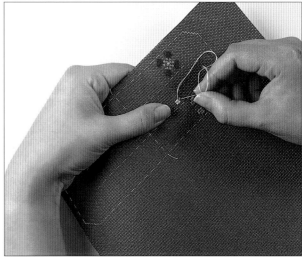

1 On the white Aida Plus fabric, baste the outline of the pattern, shown on the chart as the cutting line. Mark the two central cutting lines in the same way. The basting threads will guide you to the correct position for the stitching, and when work is complete, show you where to cut the fabric. Mark the green Aida Plus fabric in the same way.

2 Take the green Aida Plus fabric and using the loop starting method (p. 41), work all the cross stitches exactly as you would on any other Aida fabric, following all The Golden Rules of Cross Stitch (p. 117). The white Aida Plus remains unstitched and is used for the weaving (Steps 7–9, pp. 72–73).

MAKING THE BASKETS (STEPS 3 – 6)

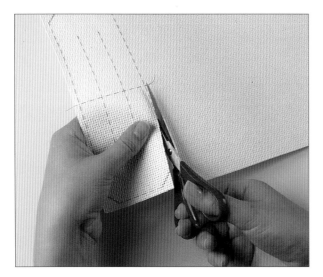

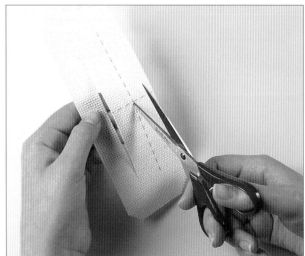

3 Using sharp, fine-pointed scissors, cut along the outer cutting line of the white Aida Plus fabric.

4 Cut along the two central cutting lines, using the fine points of the scissors to pierce the fabric at the start of each cut.

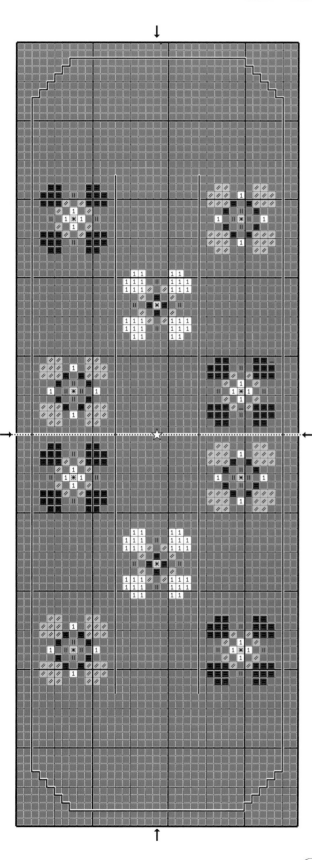

5 Repeat Steps 3 and 4 with the stitched piece of green Aida Plus.

6 Carefully fold each of the Aida Plus pieces in half, wrong sides together, along the basted fold line. Remove basting threads.

CHRISTMAS HEART-SHAPED BASKETS

Color Key

	DMC/Anchor
	Cross stitch
1 1	Blanc/1
II II	793/176
▬▬	666/335
▬	Background green fabric
⁄ ⁄	703/238
✳ ✳	726/295

—	Cutting lines
....	Folding line
☆	Middle point

NOTES

Work all cross stitches with two strands of embroidery floss.

PORCELAIN BOWL & NAPKIN HOLDER

A basket motif has been used for these items. The 1¼in (3cm) bowl lid is worked on 22-count cream Hardanger fabric using soft colors. The napkin holder is a pastel version of the one on page 68. (For charts, see p. 114.)

WEAVING THE BASKET (STEPS 7 – 9)

Holding the green fabric in your right hand and the white in your left, weave the two into a basket following the instructions and photographs below.

7 *First Row* (a) Weave the 1st white loop through the center of the 1st green loop.

(b) Weave the 2nd green loop through the center of the 1st white loop.

(c) Weave the 1st white loop through the center of the 3rd green loop.

8 *Second Row* (a) Weave the 1st green loop through the center of the 2nd white loop.

(b) Weave the 2nd white loop through the center of the 2nd green loop.

(c) Weave the 3rd green loop through the center of the 2nd white loop.

9 *Third Row* (a) Weave the 3rd white loop through the center of the 1st green loop.

(b) Weave the 2nd green loop through the center of the 3rd white loop.

(c) Weave the 3rd white loop through the center of the 3rd green loop to complete the weaving.

10 Trim the finished basket by gluing lace or braid to it, using the stitched samples pictured on page 69 as a guide. Make a hanger by adding a loop of ribbon or cord, attaching one end to the center front of the basket, and the other to the center back. Trim the center front and back with a small bow of matching ribbon. Fill with sweets or small goodies and hang on the Christmas tree.

An Expert's Secret

The properties of Aida Plus make it particularly suitable for three-dimensional projects. If you are working an Aida Plus project where the back of your work is going to be on view, you may wish to cover the back of the stitching. A second piece of Aida Plus can be ironed onto the back of your stitched work to line and stiffen it. Place both pieces of Aida Plus fabric wrong sides together, with the embroidery face down, on a thick white terry towel. Cover with a pressing cloth and iron with medium heat until the fabrics are bonded. Allow to cool flat, then check the bond and, if necessary, repeat the ironing process until a satisfactory bond is achieved. When the pieces are securely fused they can be trimmed to the desired shape.

USING WASTE CANVAS

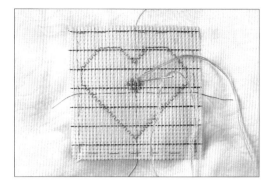

*A*ll the fabrics used so far in this book have been specially designed for counted thread embroidery, but the good news is that you are not limited to working only on speciality fabrics. Cross stitch can be worked on any fabric that can be pierced with a needle if waste canvas is first applied to the surface of that fabric. The waste canvas provides the missing holes that act as guidelines for the stitching. It is available in a variety of counts and consists of threads that are woven into an even grid, which is held rigidly in place with starch. When work is complete, the waste canvas threads are removed, leaving the stitched design on the surface of your chosen fabric.

✕ ✕ ✕ ✕

CHRISTENING GOWN

Finished Size of Heart: 2 x 1¾in (5 x 4.5cm). Stitch Count: 29 x 24

Waste canvas opens up the possibility of stitching on all manner of garments, and here a christening gown has been beautifully embellished with a floral heart cross stitch design. The more adventurous could add a name and date using back-stitch outlining (see Skill 3). An alternative patchwork heart design suitable for working on children's everyday clothes is shown on page 111 in Exploring the Options, and is charted on page 113.

You Will Need
- *Christening gown with a yoke*
- *2½ x 2½in (6.5 x 6.5cm) 14-count waste canvas*
- *Embroidery hoop (optional)*
- *Embroidery floss as in the color key*
- *Tapestry needle, size 26 (or crewel needle)*
- *Small wad of cotton*
- *Tweezers*
- *White sewing thread*
- *Trimmings to suit the gown (ribbon, roses, beads)*

HEART-SHAPED PORCELAIN BOWL
Embroidered on cream 14-count Aida, the colors have been altered to match a 3½in (9cm) porcelain bowl (chart, p. 113).

1 Carefully measure out and mark the center of the yoke on the christening gown using two intersecting lines of basting thread.

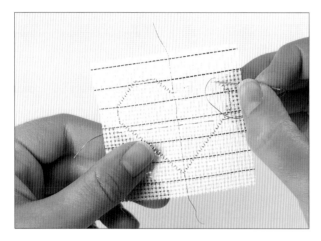

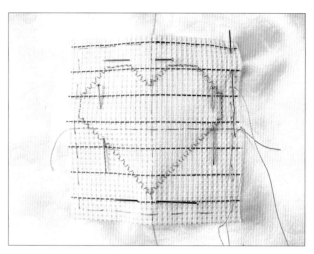

2 Using the chart to guide you, baste the outline of the heart onto the waste canvas.

3 Position the waste canvas on the yoke so that the outline of the heart is in the correct position and then baste the waste canvas to the yoke. Mount the waste canvas and yoke into an embroidery hoop, if possible (p. 17).

CHRISTENING ROBE

Color Key

	DMC/Anchor Cross stitch
⌐⌐	504/1042
⋈ ⋈	927/848
+ +	225/1026
▼ ▼	677/886
♥ ♥	778/968
◇ ◇	3743/869
—	Basting thread outline
☆	Middle point

NOTES

Work all cross stitches with three strands of embroidery floss. Use a tapestry needle if it will pierce the fabric of the gown. If not, use a crewel needle, but take care not to split or catch the waste canvas threads, as this will lead to difficulties when you come to withdraw the threads.

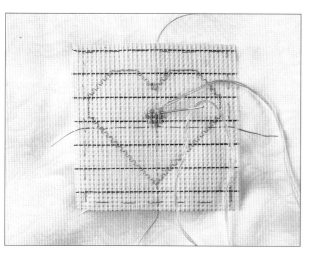

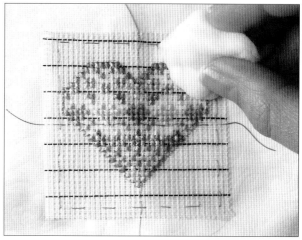

4 Using a knotless start (p. 24) and beginning with the small pink heart in the center of the design, work the cross stitch pattern, but make sure that the stitches go through both the waste canvas *and* the fabric of the gown.

5 When the embroidery is complete, dampen a wad of cotton with clean water and dab it all over the waste canvas to moisten it and thus soften the starch. This will make the threads of the canvas go limp so they are easier to remove.

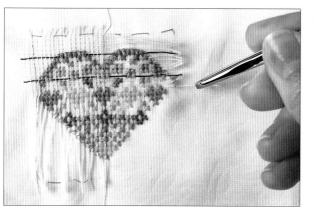

6 Using tweezers, gently pull out the threads of the waste canvas one by one, removing the basting threads as you come to them. Allow the gown to dry.

7 Using white sewing thread, decorate the gown with lace, ribbon, beads, and trimmings of your choice to complement the embroidery.

An Expert's Secret

Because you are not working on an Aida or evenweave fabric, you will have to form the holes for the stitches yourself, using the holes in the waste canvas as guides. The needle must pierce the exact center of each hole or the threads will be difficult to remove later. Where two or more stitches share the same hole, check they enter or emerge through the same hole. Working on waste canvas seems simple, but it is easy to end up with an untidy result, so work with particular care.

WORKING WITH EVENWEAVE FABRIC

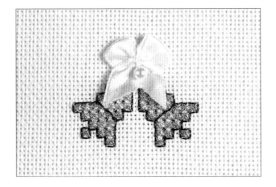

*U*nlike canvas work, where the whole of the canvas is covered with stitches that obscure the canvas, in cross stitch embroidery the background of a design is not worked. Consequently the embroidery fabric is on show and forms part of the finished work. Aida fabrics consist of blocks that form a regular square pattern, but with evenweave fabrics, such as linen, you get a smoother, less obtrusive background to your stitching. Until now you have worked the cross stitch over one block: now you will be working over two threads instead, so a thread count of 20 will produce 10 cross stitches to 1in (2.5cm). You will soon get accustomed to counting pairs of threads, rather than blocks, as you did with Aida fabrics.

✕ ✕ ✕ ✕

WEDDING PICTURE
Finished Size: 4¼ x 8in (11 x 20cm). Stitch Count: 41 x 75

For a first attempt at working on evenweave fabric, a cotton/viscose mix has been chosen with a low thread count so it will be easy to see the holes and count the pairs of threads. The chosen theme is a wedding, where the initials of your choice can be added from the alphabet provided on page 83. The wedding bells will give you your first experience with metallic thread cross stitch.

You Will Need
- *10in (25.5cm) embroidery hoop*
- *14 x 14in (35.5 x 35.5cm) 20-count Bellana evenweave fabric, in antique white*
- *Embroidery floss as in the color key*
- *DMC light silver thread*
- *Tapestry needle, size 24*
- *Small bow of white ribbon, trimmed with a pearl bead*
- *Frame of your choice, with opening larger than 4¼ x 8in (11 x 20cm)*

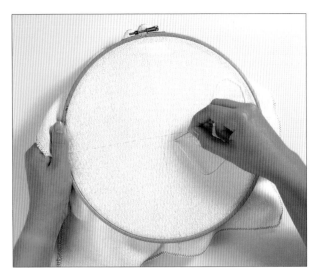

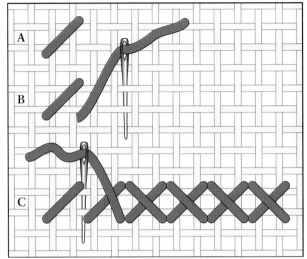

1 Prepare the fabric with basting thread (pp. 16–17) and mount it into the hoop as usual. Using a knotless start (p. 24), bring the needle to the front of the work ready to work the first stitch near the center of the design.

2 Put the needle into the fabric two threads to the right and two threads up, as shown in diagram A above. Bring the needle to the surface again two threads below as shown in diagram B above. Continue this sequence to the end of the row. Once at the end of the row, return, crossing each stitch and using the same holes as before, so that all cross stitches "hold hands" as shown in diagram C above.

This lovely wedding card has been worked on a high count fabric (see p. 112 for instructions).

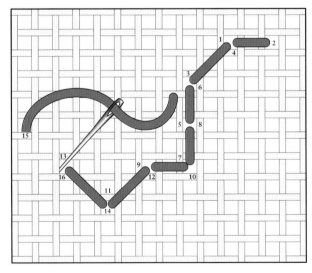

3 When the cross stitching is complete, work the backstitch outlining over two threads as shown in the diagram above. (See Skill 4 to recap backstitch outlining and also An Expert's Secret on p. 82.)

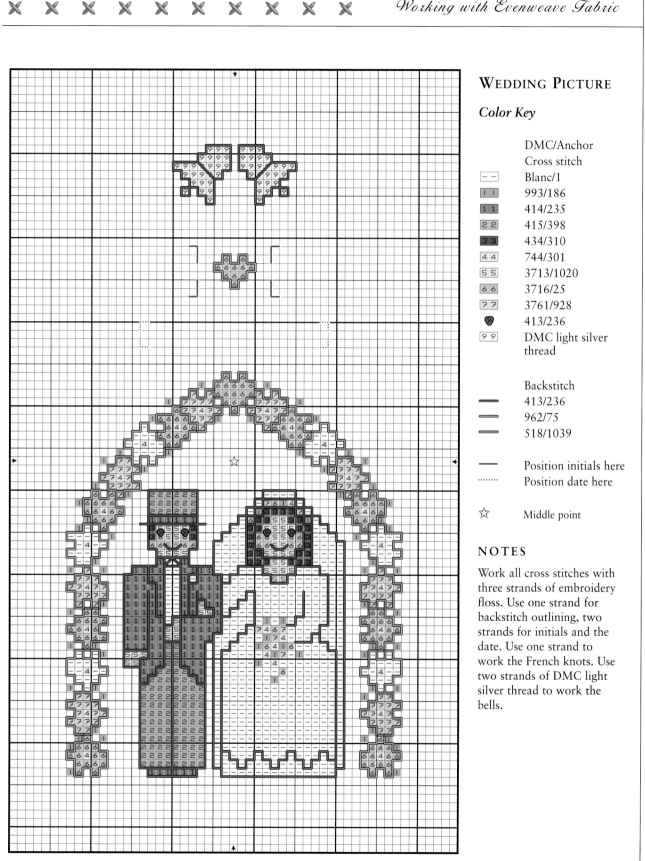

WEDDING PICTURE

Color Key

		DMC/Anchor
		Cross stitch
− −		Blanc/1
I I		993/186
1 1		414/235
2 2		415/398
3 3		434/310
4 4		744/301
5 5		3713/1020
6 6		3716/25
7 7		3761/928
⬟		413/236
9 9		DMC light silver thread

	Backstitch
——	413/236
——	962/75
——	518/1039
—	Position initials here
....	Position date here
☆	Middle point

NOTES

Work all cross stitches with three strands of embroidery floss. Use one strand for backstitch outlining, two strands for initials and the date. Use one strand to work the French knots. Use two strands of DMC light silver thread to work the bells.

An Expert's Secret

Take care when backstitching because your route may take the thread across the back of bare fabric, and with evenweave fabric this may show through an empty hole. To work the stitch illustrated in diagram 1, bring the needle out at point "b," in at "a" and out again at "c." The stitch on the back of the work may show through hole "d." To correct this, put the needle in again at "b." On the back of the work, slip the needle under the backstitch that lies between "a" and "c," as shown in diagram 2, and bring the needle to the front of the work at "e." The tension on the thread between "b" and "e" will pull the stitch into place along the edge of the embroidery at the back of the work, shown in diagram 3.

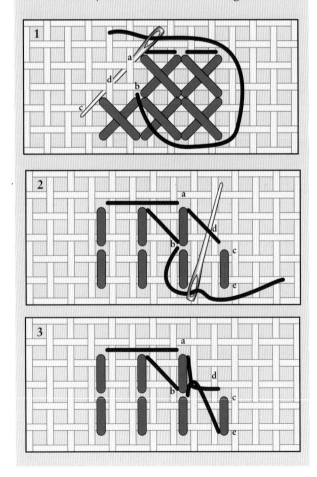

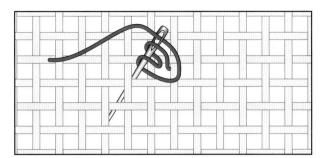

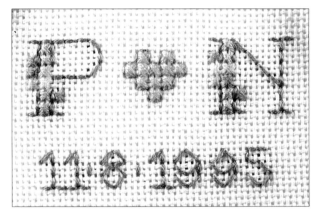

4 Work the French knots over one thread as shown in the diagram above. (See Skill 5 to recap French knots.)

5 Work the wedding date and the initials of the bride and groom as indicated on the chart on page 81, positioning them so there are four bare threads (two squares on the chart) on either side of the heart. (See Skill 3 to recap backstitch lettering.)

6 Work the bells with silver thread. Metallic thread often appears to have a mind of its own; it is springier than embroidery floss and less easy to handle, so cut shorter lengths of thread than usual to avoid tangling and fraying. This design requires two strands of silver thread to work the bells, but it is easier to work with one strand in the needle and work each stitch twice as you go, building up to a total of two strands. This makes the metallic thread easier to control and gives a better finish.

7 Remove basting. Trim the silver bells with a bow of ribbon and frame the finished work.

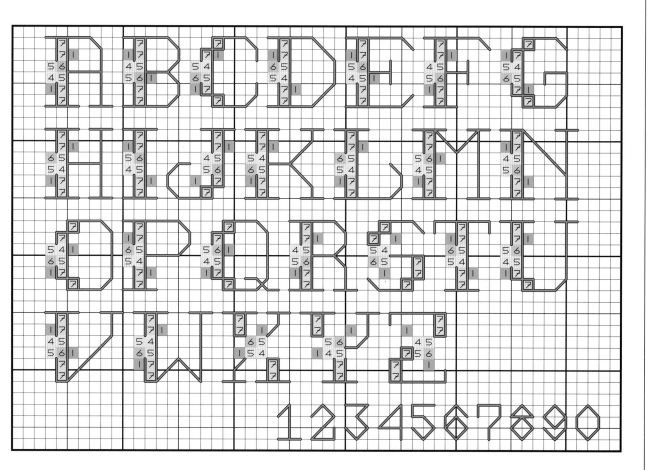

ALPHABET & NUMBERS

Color Key

DMC/Anchor
Cross stitch

1 1	993/186
4 4	744/301
5 5	3713/1020
6 6	3716/25
7 7	3761/928

Backstitch
— 992/187

NOTES

Work all cross stitches with three strands of embroidery floss. Use one strand for backstitch outlining, two strands for initials and the date.

An Expert's Secret

Counting across bare evenweave fabric can be tricky when you are finding the starting position of another part of the design. Thread a needle with some light-colored basting thread and work the first half of a cross stitch to correspond with each blank square on the chart. Continue across the bare fabric until you reach the new starting position. Check carefully that the number of half crosses matches exactly the number of blank squares on the chart. Start to cross stitch the design in the correct position and then remove the basting thread stitches.

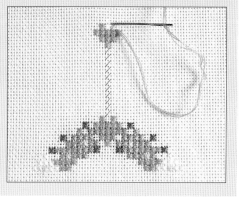

INTRODUCING
THREE-QUARTER CROSS STITCH

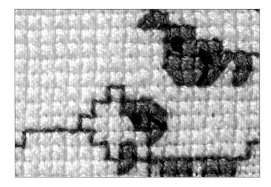

$\mathcal{N}$ow that you have graduated onto evenweave fabric it is possible to produce this fractional stitch which, when combined with full cross stitch, is used to produce more detail and the illusion of curves in very small designs. Compare the hearts on this design with the heart in the previous chapter and you will see that the "stepped" effect has been replaced with a more rounded appearance.

BIRTH ANNOUNCEMENT CARD
Finished Size: 2½ x 4¼in (6.5 x 11cm). Stitch Count: 34 x 59

Announce a birth or welcome a new baby with this design, which consists mainly of full cross stitches but features for the first time the occasional three-quarter cross stitch. Pastel colors have been used for this design, so you may like to consider stitching with DMC flower thread for an even softer effect.

You Will Need
- *6in (15cm) embroidery hoop*
- *10 x 10in (25.5 x 25.5cm) 28-count Jobelan evenweave fabric, in white*
- *Embroidery floss or flower thread as in the color key*
- *Tapestry needle, size 26*
- *Greeting card with a 2¾ x 4½in (7 x 11.5cm) mat opening*
- *Dressmaking scissors*

- *Paper-cutting scissors or craft knife and metal ruler*
- *Double-sided tape*
- *Small cardboard carton*
- *Scrap paper*
- *Spray adhesive*
- *⅛in (3cm) wide ribbon to trim card*

Opposite *This design can also be made up into a wall hanging (for full instructions see p. 112).*

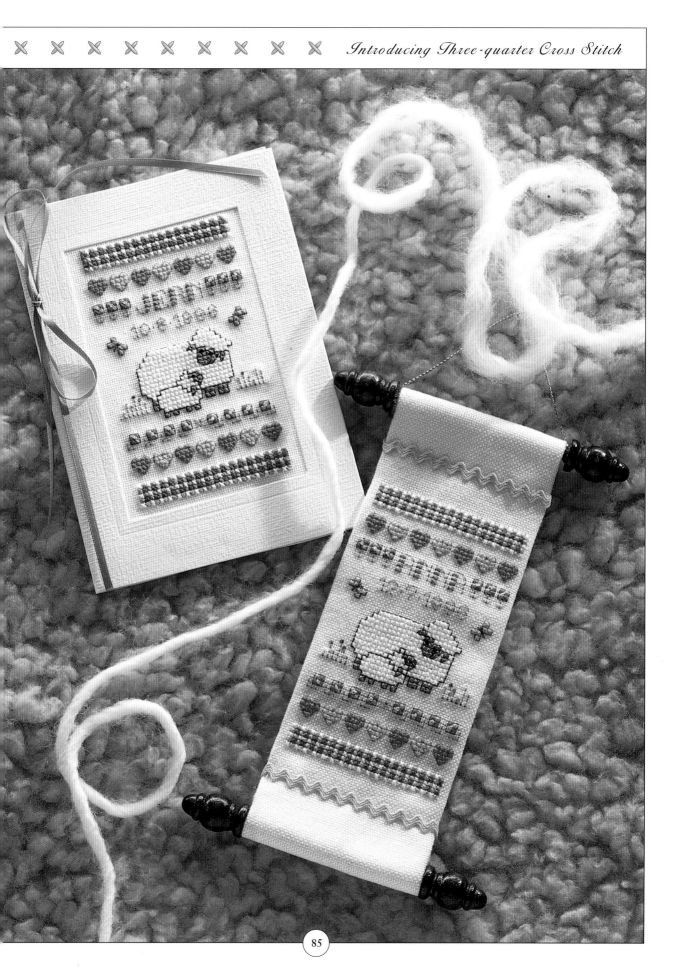

THREE-QUARTER CROSS STITCH

Because stitches on evenweave fabrics are worked over two threads you have a total of nine holes in the space of one full cross stitch (see diagram A, below). The center hole (5), non-existent on an Aida block, makes it possible to work a three-quarter cross stitch. Full cross stitch forms a square shape, and three-quarter cross stitch forms two adjacent right angled triangles (see diagrams B and C, below).

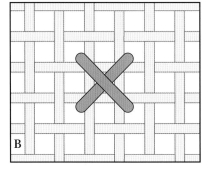

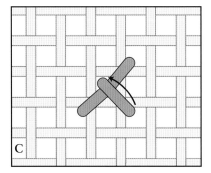

1 Prepare the fabric and mount it into a hoop (pp. 16–17). Following the chart and using the loop starting method (p. 41), work the cross stitches. A square shape on the chart indicates a full cross stitch. A symbol in a right-angled triangle indicates that you should work a three-quarter stitch as follows. Work the first half of the cross stitch as usual in the direction indicated by the slope on the triangle symbol on the chart (the diagrams below illustrate how the chart symbols translate into stitches). Work the second stitch over the top of the first stitch and bring the needle down into the center hole, as shown above right. (This will sometimes break the Golden Rule of always having the top stitch lying in the same direction, but it is necessary that the top stitch neatly anchors the bottom one by passing over the top of it, as shown in the detail photograph below.)

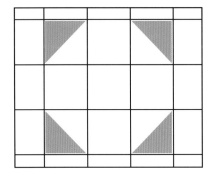

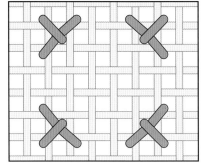

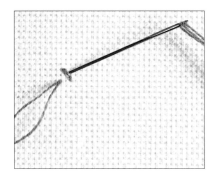

An Expert's Secret

When working three-quarter cross stitches, do not pull the first stitch tight before working the quarter stitch, as this will obscure the hole into which you work the quarter stitch. Leave the first stitch slack, exposing the center hole, insert the needle into the center hole and stop. Now pull the first stitch tight and complete the second stitch as normal.

BIRTH ANNOUNCEMENT CARD

Color Key

DMC/Anchor/Flower Thread

1 1	Blanc/1/Blanc
2 2	746/275/Ecru
3 3	414/235/2414
	809/130/2799
	798/131/2798
	552/99/2532
◇ ◇	554/96/2210
● ●	603/62/2899
T T	605/50/2776
- -	993/186/2952
	992/187/2956
	413/236/2413
	310/403/2310
	744/301/2743

——	Position name or initials here
....	Position date here
☆	Middle point

NOTES

Work all cross stitches with two strands of embroidery floss or flower thread. Use one strand to work backstitches and French knots.

A square shape on the chart represents the use of a full cross stitch. A right-angled triangle on the chart indicates the use of a three-quarter cross stitch. Two right-angled triangles occupying the same square indicates that two three-quarter cross stitches should be worked back to back (see Step 3, p. 88).

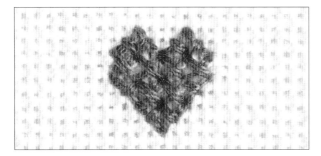

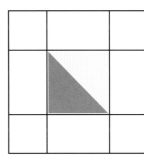

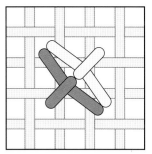

2 When working the hearts (above) you will find that they include the three-quarter cross stitch in all of its four possible positions (see diagram below).

3 Where two three-quarter stitches occupy the space of a full cross stitch they must be worked back to back, sharing the center hole. This occurs when you work the ears and noses on the sheep.

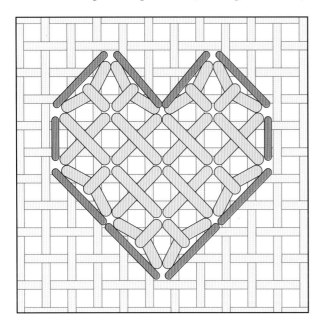

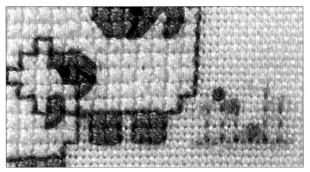

4 Work the French knot "flowers." (See Skill 5 to recap French knots.) Space has been left on the chart so that you can personalize your work with a short name or initials and a date, using the alphabet and numbers provided. (See Skill 3 to recap backstitch lettering.)

MOUNTING EMBROIDERY IN A CARD (STEPS 5 – 10)

When the embroidery is complete you are ready to mount the work into a card. Greeting cards are readily available in an enormous variety of colors, shapes, and sizes with precut mats for your finished work.

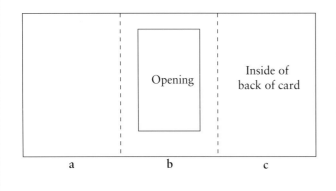

5 Establish which is the top and which is the bottom of the card. For example, look at section "b" in the diagram, left. At the top of the card the border around the opening is narrower than the border at the bottom of the card. You may want to turn the card so the narrow border is at the bottom.

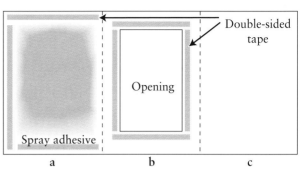

a   b   c

Double-sided tape

Opening

Spray adhesive

6 Check that the card folds shut without gaping. If necessary cut a thin sliver of card off section "a" to make it shut correctly. Use paper-cutting scissors for this, or, better still, a sharp craft knife held against a steel ruler. When using a craft knife, protect the surface on which you are cutting with several layers of cardboard or a cutting mat.

8 Lay the embroidery face up on a flat surface. Remove the backing strips from the double-sided tape. Hold the card face up and position the opening around the embroidery, checking that the work is straight and centered; press the embroidery onto the tape. Do not worry if you do not get it right the first time, as the double-sided tape will allow you to make several attempts.

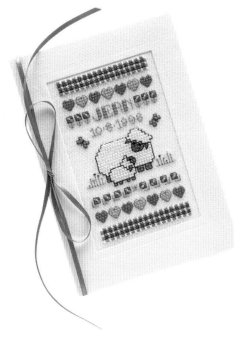

7 Using dressmaking scissors, trim the embroidery to fit the opening, leaving ½in (1.25cm) spare fabric all round. Using paper-cutting scissors, cut lengths of double-sided tape to fit around the opening and section "a" (see diagram above). On the inside of the card stick the lengths of double-sided tape in the positions shown.

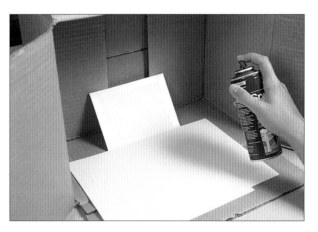

9 Place the card, right side down, in a small carton, mask off sections "b" and "c" with scrap paper and spray a squirt of spray adhesive onto section "a." The carton and scrap paper will stop the adhesive from going where it is not wanted and the spray adhesive will give the embroidery a sticky surface onto which to cling without rippling.

10 Fold section "a" over section "b," stroke down firmly and write your message on section "c." Trim with a length of fine ribbon tied around the front of the card.

ADVANCED
THREE-QUARTER CROSS STITCH

Extensive use of three-quarter cross stitch in all its forms is made in this design, offering you plenty of practice in fractional stitching. This chapter also introduces you to tweeding, a subtle method of shading, where two different colors of embroidery floss are used together in the needle.

FAMILY TREE

Finished Size: 4¾ x 4¾in (12 x 12cm). Stitch Count: 66 x 64

Three generations are represented on this family tree, which is adaptable to everybody's circumstances. Simply change the initials to suit the family history using the alphabet supplied. Photocopy the design and draw the required initials in the spaces on the chart. Place the grandparents' initials on the top line, the parents' initials on the second, and the child's initials on the bottom line. The border is composed of apples at various stages of maturity to reflect the different ages pictured on the family tree.

You Will Need
- *8in (20cm) embroidery hoop*
- *12 x 12in (30.5 x 30.5cm) 27-count Linda evenweave fabric, in antique white*
- *Embroidery floss as in the color key*
- *Tapestry needle, size 26*
- *Jewelry links (optional)*
- *Frame of choice*

Place an initial on either side of the French knots

1 Prepare the fabric for work (p. 16) and mount into the hoop (p. 17). Using the loop starting method (p. 41), stitch over two threads of the fabric. Work the full and the three-quarter stitches first, then the backstitches and French knots.

TWEEDING (STEPS 2 – 4)

The ripening apples in the border are worked with two shades of stranded cotton. Where orange, for example, changes to yellow a row of "tweeding" is worked to soften the transition and give a more natural effect. This is achieved quite simply by working the stitches with one strand of orange thread and one strand of yellow thread in the needle. The rest of the two-toned apples are worked in the same way, using the shades given in the color key.

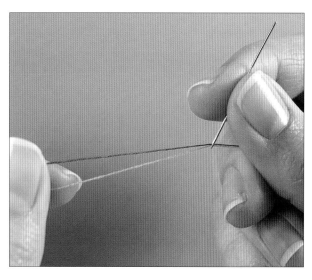

2 Thread the needle with two different color threads.

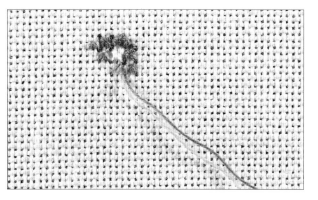

3 Work full and three-quarter cross stitches with the mixed color thread (see An Expert's Secret, p. 94).

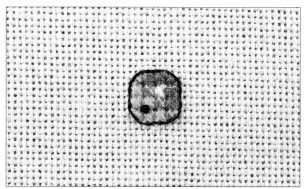

4 Finish stitching the two-tone apple and carefully outline it in backstitch. (See Skill 4 to recap backstitch outlining.)

FAMILY TREE
Color Key

DMC/Anchor			
Cross stitch	9 9	445/288	1 strand each of:
▦▦ 300/352	‖ ‖	809/130	⊞ ⊞ 742/303 + 946/332
1 1 Blanc/1	▬▬	498/1005	↖ ↖ 704/256 + 445/288
2 2 746/275	⋗ ⋗	318/399	✳ ✳ 445/288 + 742/303
5 5 946/332	╱╱	797/132	
6 6 948/6	△ △	700/228	Backstitch French knot
7 7 754/8	▬▬	702/226	—— 310/403 ❥ 310/403
8 8 742/303	╱╱	704/256	—— 498/1005
	◖◗	310/403	—— 797/132 ☆ Middle point

NOTES

Work all cross stitches with two strands of embroidery floss. Use one strand for backstitches and French knots.

An Expert's Secret

In order to achieve the best coverage possible of the fabric when working with two strands of cotton, try a technique called "railroading." Before inserting your needle into the hole in the fabric, separate the two strands of cotton coming from the previous hole and pass the needle between the two strands as it enters the next hole. This serves to separate the strands, remove any twists from them, and ensure that they lie neatly side by side.

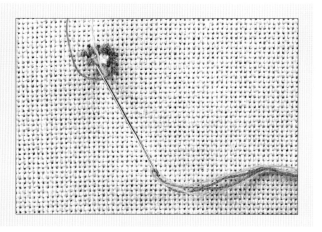

DEPICTING CHARACTER DETAILS (STEPS 5 – 6)

5 The people portrayed at the bottom of the design can be altered to look more like the actual people they represent. Height, hair color and style, clothing, and footwear can all be altered as necessary, and jewelry links can be stitched to faces for eyeglass wearers. Skin tone can be changed by choosing a thread color that more closely matches the person you are stitching, and a beard can easily be indicated (see the character on the far right of the photograph above). If you want to show the profession of a person, the outfits can be changed to suit. Adapt the clothing to suggest a uniform and add details such as a doctor's bag or a briefcase for a business person. With a little practice you will find that it is relatively simple to create your own unique characters.

6 When the embroidery is complete, remove it from the hoop and take out basting threads. Press if necessary (p. 30). Frame according to your choice.

WORKING WITH SILK GAUZE

*T*his chapter is for those of you who think that small is beautiful, as working with silk gauze gives stitchers the opportunity to work on a very tiny scale. Silk gauze, an even-count mono canvas consisting of single threads woven together, is made with raw silk fibers, and is ideal for jewelry, doll house projects, and miniature framed pictures. It holds its shape while work is in progress, so no hoop is required, and it will not fray or need stretching after work is completed. It can be purchased in rolls if you plan to do a lot of this work, or in small squares that are conveniently mounted into a cardboard frame. You do need to be able to see the holes clearly if you are going to enjoy working on silk gauze and there are many aids on the market to help—from eyeglasses to special magnifiers.

✖ ✖ ✖ ✖

ZODIAC JEWELRY

Finished Size: 1¼ x 1in (3 x 2.5cm). Stitch Count: 41 x 31

Why not stitch your own birth sign or treat a friend to a very special birthday present?

The silk gauze chosen for your first attempt has 32 holes to 1in (2.5cm). Much finer silk gauze is available, and for more ambitious later efforts try working on a 50-count. Once you have adjusted to the small scale of the work you should find that working on silk gauze is as simple as working on Aida fabric. Each stitch is worked over one thread of the gauze.

Madeira silk embroidery floss has been chosen to work the Zodiac designs, as one strand of the floss is just the right thickness to give good coverage of the gauze. Balger blending filament was chosen to work the gold stars because it is the "twinkliest" gold thread available.

You Will Need
• One 3½in (9cm) square of 32-count silk gauze (sufficient to work four designs)

• Madeira silk embroidery floss, in black and white
• Metallic gold blending filament
• Two tapestry needles, size 26
• Oval gilt-plated jewelry mount, 1½ x 1⅛in (3.8 x 2.8cm)
• Gilt-plated chain for pendant or bow fob for brooch
• Spray adhesive

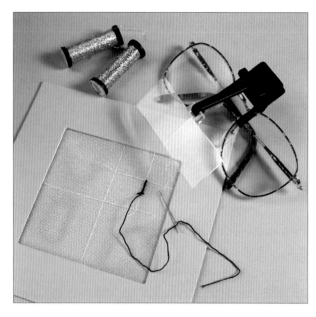

A magnifier that clips onto eyeglasses is a great help with fine work.

1 Start by dividing your square of silk gauze into four equal squares using basting threads. Next subdivide one of the squares into four using basting thread to find the center of the square (p. 17).

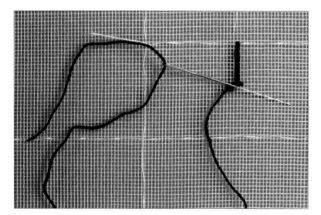

2 Thread one needle with one strand of black floss and the other needle with one strand of white floss. Starting with a knotless start (p. 24), work the design in the center of the square, using all the usual techniques for starting, cross stitching, and finishing. Work all stitches over one thread of the gauze.

4 Choose with great care the route that your cross stitch takes. Because the gauze is so transparent, never carry the thread over a part of the design that is not solidly stitched.

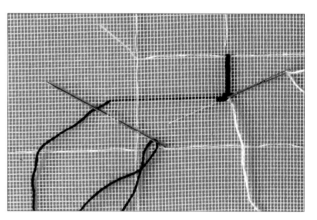

3 When you come to a white stitch, work it immediately alongside the black stitch, as you will not be able to see the gaps to fill in the white stitches later. Thus you will have two needles in use in the areas where there are white stitches. Keep the thread that is not working tucked to one side on the back of the gauze, out of the way until needed.

Opposite *The charted Zodiac designs on pages 100–101 provide a perfect introduction to working with silk gauze; but they can just as easily be worked on Aida fabric too. See page 99 for details.*

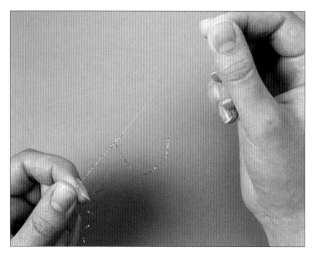

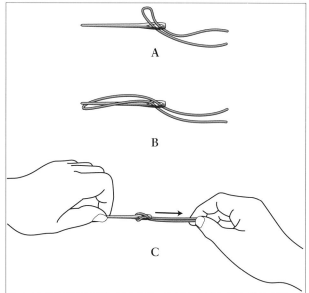

5 When working the stars, try this new method of working with metallic thread to get the best possible results from a very springy thread. Cut a 12in (30.5cm) length of gold thread. Stroke it to loosen the inner nylon thread then remove and discard the nylon thread. This leaves a thread that resembles fine gold tinsel, which will be easier to control when working on such a small scale.

6 Fold the gold thread in half to form a loop, pass the loop through the eye of the needle (A) and pass the needle through the loop (B) so that the thread is knotted onto the needle (C). Again, this gives you more control.

An Expert's Secret

Starting and finishing neatly can be tricky when a tiny patch of cross stitches stand alone, as in the case of many of the stars in these Zodiac designs. Just follow this simple technique for perfect results. Knot the end of the thread and insert the needle into the surface of the gauze several inches away from the star. A few inches of thread have to be wasted but the sacrifice is worth making for a neat finish. Work the five cross stitches and the backstitch "twinkles," which will provide a few stitches on the back of the work into which the thread can be neatly woven and

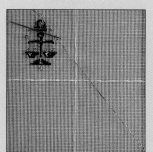

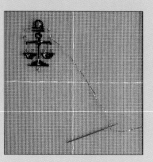

finished off (left). Trim the finished ends neatly. Cut off the knot from the starting thread and take it to the back of the work. Rethread the needle with the starting thread (below left) and weave the thread into the back of the existing stitches. Trim the ends again and, bingo. . . a star in the middle of bare fabric with no threads trailing to nearby stitching to spoil the finished appearance.

This technique can be used for a perfect finish in other designs where single cross stitches appear, for example, in borders, sprigged wallpaper, or a night sky.

The Zodiac designs could just as easily be stitched on Aida as silk gauze. All the designs fit neatly into the lid of an oval $2^7/8$ x 2in (7.3 x 5cm) porcelain bowl, if worked on 16-count, but the white stitches are not worked, leaving the fabric showing.

To stitch a Zodiac sign birthday card (see Zodiac card, p. 97) work on cream 16-count Aida to fit a card with an oval opening $3^3/8$ x $2^1/2$in (8.6 x 6.5cm). The background fabric is left bare, and gold paper stars can be stuck to the front to echo the design. (See Mounting Embroidery in a Card, pp. 88–89.)

7 Before making your first stitch with the gold thread, dampen it slightly, as this subdues it still further. Either pull the needle and thread through a piece of damp sponge, or use the quicker, but admittedly less hygienic, method of sucking it.

MOUNTING THE WORK IN A JEWELRY MOUNT

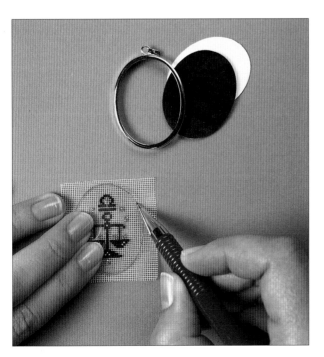

8 When work is complete, remove the basting threads and cut the stitched design from the cardboard frame. Supplied with the jewelry mount are an acetate disk, a paper disk, and a backing disk, together with instructions. Lay the acetate disk over the stitching so that the design is centered. Mark around the edge with a pencil and carefully cut the gauze along the pencil line so that it fits the mount. Spray the oval paper disk with spray adhesive and stick the wrong size of the gauze to the paper disk, again ensuring that the design is centered. The adhesive will prevent the gauze from rippling when mounted. Place the acetate sheet into the mount, then insert the embroidery on the paper disk, and lastly place the backing disk. Press down the metal tabs at the back of the mount to hold the backing disk in place and hang your mounted work from a chain or a bow fob.

ZODIAC JEWELRY

Color Key

Cross stitch
- ▬ ▬ Madeira silk embroidery floss: black
- ☐ ☐ Metallic blending filament: 002 gold
- 1 1 Madeira silk embroidery floss: white

Backstitch
- ▬▬▬ Madeira silk embroidery floss: black
- ▬▬▬ Shape of mount
- ══ Metallic blending filament: 002 gold

NOTES

Work all cross stitches with one strand of silk floss. Use two strands of gold blending filament to work the stars. Work all stitches over one thread of the gauze.

ZODIAC SIGNS

1 AQUARIUS (21 January–19 February)

2 PISCES (20 February–20 March)

3 ARIES (21 March–20 April)

4 TAURUS (21 April–22 May)

5 GEMINI (23 May–21 June)

6 CANCER (22 June–22 July)

7 LEO (23 July–22 August)

8 VIRGO (23 August–22 September)

9 LIBRA (23 September–22 October)

10 SCORPIO (23 October–21 November)

11 SAGITTARIUS (22 November–22 December)

12 CAPRICORN (23 December–20 January)

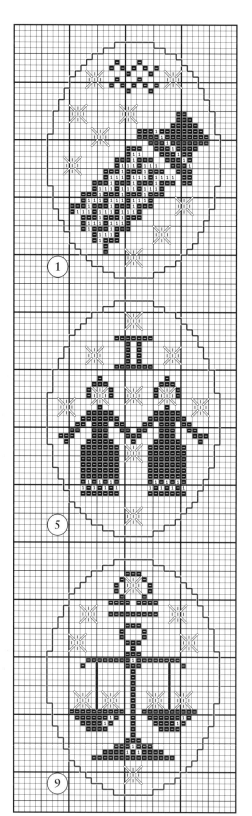

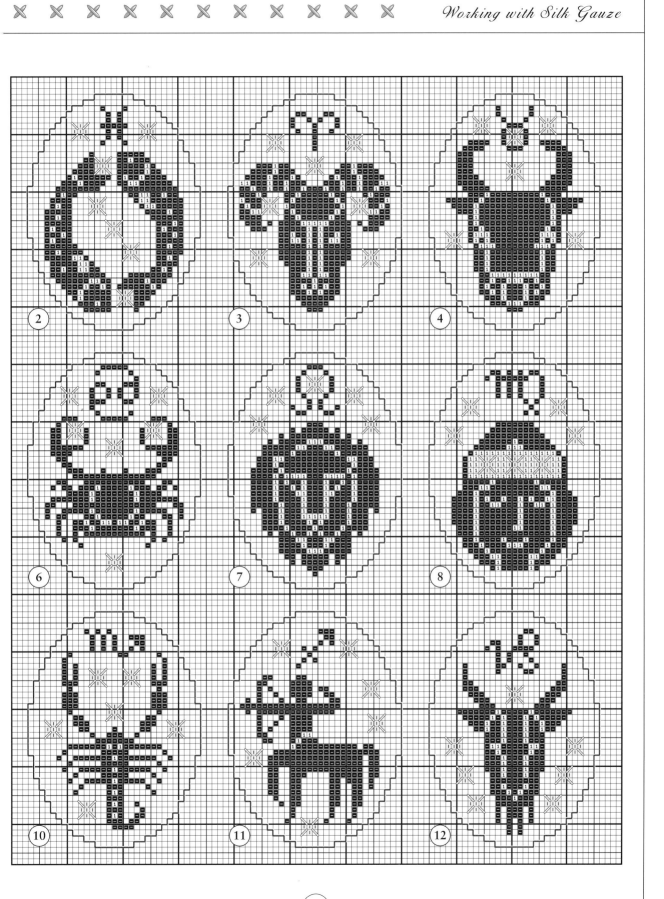

ORNAMENTED CROSS STITCH

*N*ow that you have perfected all the techniques of cross stitch you may wish to add texture and sparkle to your work by incorporating ribbons, beads, lace and sequins into the stitching. Not only can ribbons be couched with cross stitches to the surface of the fabric,

where they form lines of solid color, but they can also be further ornamented with seed beads. Larger beads can add texture and color, while sequins provide sparkle. To add froth, lace can be applied to the surface of the fabric by cross stitching along the straight edge of the lace.

X X X X

TEXTURED SAMPLER
Finished Size: This will depend on your frame

Choose a pretty frame and fill it with rows of the pattern to make a delectable sampler. When you have mastered the techniques you could stitch favorite rows onto small pieces of fabric to mount as greeting cards. Try changing the color scheme and choice of ornamentation—the possibilities are endless.

I worked my sampler on 22-count Oslo Hardanger fabric in cream, but you may prefer to choose a different evenweave fabric. Quantities for the ornamentation will depend on the

size of your frame.

The frame can be painted to match your embroidery; spray it outdoors with spray paint.

You Will Need
- *Frame for the finished work*
- *Evenweave fabric, sufficient to fill the frame plus 2in (5cm) all round for turning*
- *Embroidery hoop (large enough to contain the whole design)*
- *Embroidery floss as in the color key*
- *Tapestry needles, sizes 24 and 26*
- *Beading needle, size 10*

- *White sewing cotton*
- *Glass seed beads: blue, cream, green, and pink*
- *⅛in (3mm) wide mauve ribbon*
- *½in (1.25cm) wide white cotton lace, (choose a lace with regular holes along the straight edge)*
- *³⁄₁₆in (5mm) opalescent heart-shaped beads*
- *³⁄₁₆in (5mm) white rickrack*
- *³⁄₁₆in (5mm) silver star-shaped sequins*
- *Pearl beading*

1 Prepare the fabric for work and mount it in the hoop. *Row 1* Using a knotless start (p. 24) and size 24 tapestry needle, and starting with the large hearts, work straightforward cross stitch.

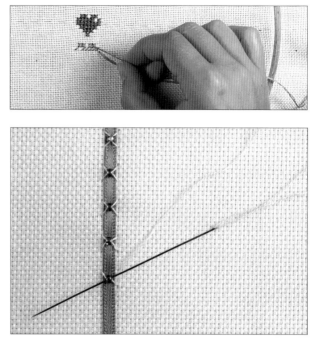

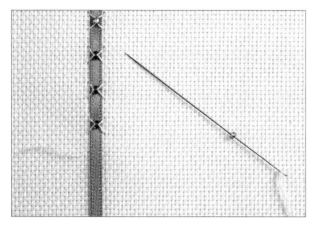

2 *Row 2* Cut a length of ribbon and place it lengthwise on the fabric. Using a beading needle and one strand of cream embroidery floss bring the needle out at the correct position, as shown on the chart, to one side of the ribbon. Thread a blue seed bead onto the floss and insert the needle into the correct position on the other side of the ribbon to

3 *Row 3* Work straightforward cross stitch and backstitch for the trailing flowers.

form the first half of a large cross stitch. Bring the needle out again, ready to complete the cross stitch. Put the needle through the seed bead again in the opposite direction and pass over the ribbon to complete the stitch. The ribbon is now couched to the surface of the fabric and the couching cross stitch is embellished with a seed bead.

An Expert's Secret

When stitching with a beading needle you will find that the fine, sharp point of the needle is prone to split the threads of the fabric. In order to ensure that the thread is delivered to the hole correctly, try working with the beading needle upside down. This entails working with the threaded eye of the needle, and care is needed to avoid pricking oneself with the sharp end.

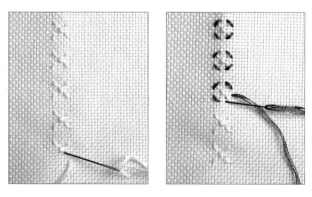

4 *Row 4* On each repeat, work the center cross stitch followed by diagonal stitches at each corner using three strands of cream embroidery floss. Then, using three strands of blue floss, cross each of the corner stitches to form bi-colored cross stitches.

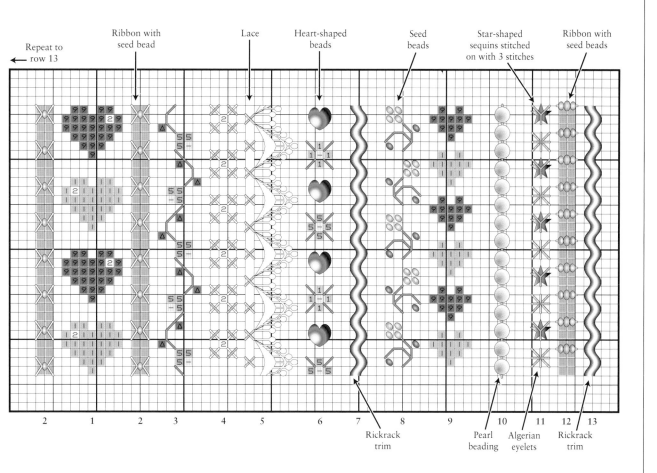

Repeat to ← row 13

Ribbon with seed bead

Lace

Heart-shaped beads

Seed beads

Star-shaped sequins stitched on with 3 stitches

Ribbon with seed beads

2 1 2 3 4 5 6 7 8 9 10 11 12 13

Rickrack trim

Pearl beading

Algerian eyelets

Rickrack trim

TEXTURED SAMPLER

Color Key

	DMC/Anchor Cross stitch
＋＋	677/886
｜｜	932/1033
1 1	3727/1016
2 2	712/926
5 5	3042/870
9 9	931/1034
△△	502/876
▦	Ribbon

—	502/876
—	712/926
—	316/1017
—	932/1033

NOTES

Work all cross stitches with three strands of embroidery floss. Use two strands for backstitch and one strand for beads and sequins.

Work enough of each row of the pattern to fill your frame. Check that your rows are long enough by holding the frame face down on the work as each row nears completion. Be generous with the number of repeats you work, even if some of your work is swallowed up in the framing; it is better to have too much than not enough to fill the frame.

When one side of the pattern is complete, work the mirror image to fill the other half of the design.

5 *Row 5* Using three strands of pink embroidery floss, stitch the white cotton lace to the fabric using cross stitches at regular intervals along the straight edge of the lace.

6 *Row 6* Stitch the flowers in cross stitch and backstitch. Attach the heart-shaped beads between the flowers using one strand of cream embroidery floss.

7 *Row 7* Stitch a length of white rickrack into position using white sewing cotton and tiny, invisible backstitches.

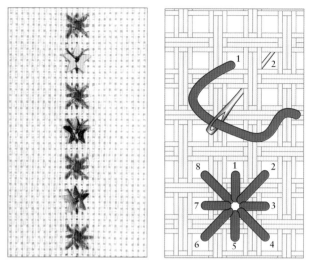

11 *Row 11* Attach the star-shaped sequins using one strand of blue embroidery floss and the size 26 tapestry needle. Work three straight stitches into the center hole of each sequin as shown on the chart. Work Algerian eyelets between the sequins, using two strands of pink floss. Work each stitch in turn, starting at 1, into the center hole (see diagram above). Tug slightly on the thread after each stitch to slightly enlarge the hole and produce a lacy effect.

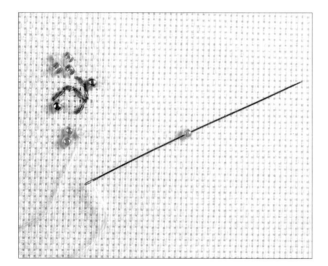

8 *Row 8* Using a beading needle and one strand of cream stranded cotton, stitch the seed beads into the positions shown on the chart. Use half cross stitches to attach them and, to ensure that all the beads lie in the same direction, be consistent in the direction of stitching the half cross stitches.

9 *Row 9* Stitch the small hearts following the chart, using straightforward cross stitch.

10 *Row 10* Using three strands of pink embroidery floss, couch a length of pearl beading to the fabric with cross stitches at regular intervals between pearls.

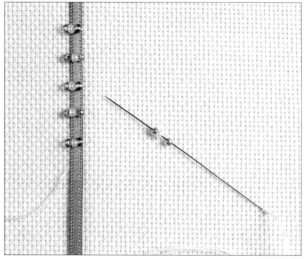

12 *Row 12* Work as Step 2 (Row 2), but for variety couch the ribbon with straight stitches holding three seed beads.

13 *Row 13* Repeat Step 7 (Row 7), stitching a length of white rickrack into position using white sewing thread and tiny backstitches.

14 When all the stitching is complete, remove the work from the hoop and frame it in your chosen frame.

TARTAN CHRISTMAS FRAME

Revamp the textured design by stitching on 22-count Hardanger in Christmas red. Follow the instructions for working the heart-shaped frame but substitute a circular green frame and Christmas-colored threads (see chart, p. 115). Tiny jingle bells replace the heart-shaped beads, and tartan ribbon, gathered into a ruffle, is glued to the back of the frame.

EXPLORING THE OPTIONS

There are many ways to display your cross stitch embroidery, both decorative and functional. Being familiar with a variety of finishing and mounting techniques will enable you to put your cross stitch patterns to more than one use, thus expanding your repertoire and getting extra value from the designs. A design for a picture may be suitable for mounting as a card, or a portion of the design might make a delightful bowl lid or bookmark. Equally, a simple change of color scheme can give a design a whole new appearance. Throughout the book I have suggested ideas and provided instructions for adapting the designs so that completely new items can be made. (These are also referred to below.) The charts for these additional projects are provided on pages 113–116. All of the adaptations are easy to do if you follow the guidelines in this chapter. The secret is to look for the potential in a design and explore the options to exploit it to the full.

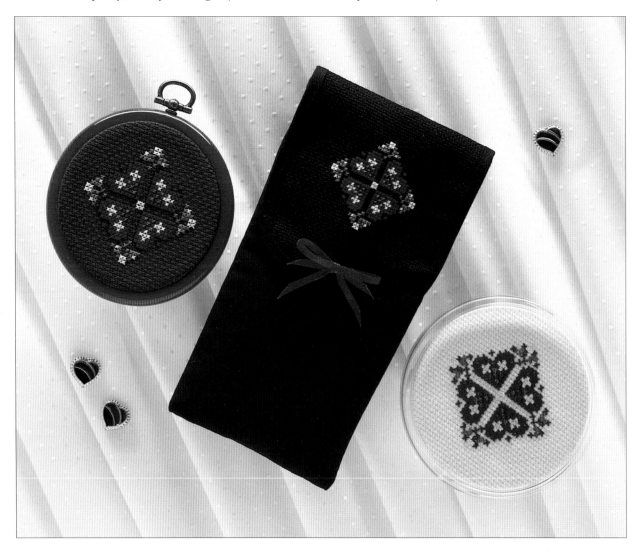

CHANGING THE FABRIC COLOR

The simplest way to give a design a whole new look is to change the color of the background fabric, and there is a wonderfully wide range of fabric colors available nowadays. See what a contrast there is between the blue and white needle cases on pages 23 and 29. The Tartan Christmas Frame (p. 107), a version of the Textured Sampler (p.103), also shows how effective changing the fabric color can be.

CHANGING THE STITCHING COLORS

With so many lovely shades at your disposal do not feel constrained to stick to the color key provided for a design. For a whole new look, try substituting your own colors. (Advice on choosing colors is given on p. 32.) The ruler on page 41 was redesigned using motifs from the First Sampler design (p. 40) and bright primary colors were used to appeal to a child. Elements of the Bookmark design (p. 36) were also reworked and recolored for a towel border (p. 37). The magnetic note holder (p. 35) could be customized to match your kitchen decor.

CUSTOMIZING & ADAPTING DESIGNS

You can also customize and adapt charts to make them more personal and suitable for your circumstances. The scope here is almost limitless.

Opposite Here, the adaptability of a design is illustrated. The central portion of the Treasure Box design (p. 65) has been given three completely different looks for three very different items—a coaster, an eyeglass case, and a flexi-hoop picture. All three are worked from the same chart (p. 116). Both the coaster and the eyeglass case are available commercially ready-to-use. The standard 3¼in (8cm) coaster was worked on cream 14-count Aida (see page 111 for finishing instructions). The eyeglass case was worked in bright colors on an 18-count black Aida flap incorporated into the fabric, which gives a wonderful folk art look to the design. A small red ribbon bow has been added to finish.

Washing Cross Stitch

You will need to wash the work before mounting it if it has become grubby. First test for color fastness. Work a few stitches of each color on a fabric scrap and wash as usual. If none of the colors run it is safe to wash the embroidery. Use soap suds and lukewarm water and gently swish the stitching around. Do not rub or twist, as you may distort the stitches. Use several changes of clear, tepid water to rinse, then lay the embroidery to dry on a clean, white terry towel, before pressing it (p. 30).

Names and dates can be added as shown in the First Sampler on page 39. Or by repositioning elements of one design a whole new pattern can appear (see the key tag and ruler on p. 41, both adapted from the First Sampler design).

To create your own design you will need graph paper, 10 squares to 1in (2.5cm) is best, and a pencil to chart it out before you start stitching. Use the graph paper to copy out motifs or names and dates to personalize your work. Later you may want to design your own samplers, pictures, and cards.

Key Tag

Several of the motifs in the sampler on page 39 have been placed together to make a new design that will fit a key tag—an ideal present for someone moving to a new house. Follow the chart on page 115 and work on 14-count Rustico Aida. Back with iron-on interfacing to hide the stitching and prevent fraying. Cut the design to size and mount into the key tag.

Ruler

Motifs from the sampler on page 39 have again been combined to produce a fresh design, this time to fit a ruler. Using the chart on pages 114–115, stitch on white perforated paper (see Skill 7 to recap working with perforated paper). Using the cover of the ruler as a guide, cut out a piece of plain, white backing paper to fit. Similarly, cut the perforated paper to fit the opening. Place the backing paper in the ruler, then the embroidery, face up. Snap one end of the cover into place, bend the cover (it is flexible), and slot the other end into place. The flatter your work is on the wrong side, the better the fit.

FRAMING YOUR WORK

Designs that are designated as greeting cards, potpourri sachets, and other unprotected stitching, can all be framed for wall display. A complementary choice of frame can enhance a design and give it a totally new look, as can be seen in the Lavender Sachet Bag design on page 54. It is best to choose a framer who specializes in framing embroidery. Ensure that the work will be mounted onto acid-free card to prevent "foxing" (small brown spots that appear in time, mark the fabric, and ruin its appearance).

Use a mat wherever possible to prevent the glass from flattening the surface of the embroidery, or ask the framer to raise the glass by placing thin strips of card around the edges of the frame where the overlap will hide them. Use plain or nonreflective glass, whichever you prefer, but plain glass gives a better view of your masterpiece. Avoid hanging framed work in full sun because the bright light will fade the threads and rot the fabric.

Flexi-hoop Picture

A flexi-hoop can be used as a decorative frame as shown on page 108. Here the Treasure Box design has been adapted and worked on navy 14-count Aida to fit a 3in (7.5cm) red flexi-hoop. The fabric was cut to a 5 x 5in (13 x 13cm) piece and laid over the inner hoop. The outer hoop was eased over the fabric and the inner hoop until it snapped into place, making sure that the threads of the fabric were straight in relation to the hanger at the top of the hoop. When the work was complete, the excess fabric was trimmed to ½in (1.25cm). A fine running

stitch was worked around the edge of the fabric, and the thread pulled up to draw the gathers toward the center of the back of the flexi-hoop. The threads were finished off tautly. The back of the work was covered by gluing on a circle of felt.

USING COMMERCIAL MOUNTS

A glance through a mount supplier's catalog will spark many new ideas for presenting your work—key tags, napkin holders, bowls, cards, coasters, paperweights—the list is excitingly long. But before rushing to place an order, check that your chosen design will fit the mount (see p. 12). There are several examples throughout the book of these commercially made products, such as the napkin holder on page 68, derived from the Christmas Heart-shaped Baskets design. More ideas follow on using some of the mounts available commercially.

Bowl Lids

Bowls in all shapes and sizes, in porcelain, glass, wood, or metal are available nowadays. The lids are supplied as blanks and can be filled with pressed flowers, lace, or embroidery. Examples in this book are the tiny porcelain bowl design, adapted from the Christmas Heart-shaped Baskets (p. 71); the heart-shaped porcelain bowl (p. 74) and the oval porcelain bowl (p. 99) using the Zodiac designs from pages 100–101.

Manufacturers normally provide instructions for mounting embroidery into bowl lids, but instructions are also provided here. Generally, you will first need to back your stitched piece with iron-on interfacing, to prevent fraying when you cut the work to fit the lid. Along with the bowl and lid, most manufacturers supply an acetate disk, a sponge disk, a paper disk, a metal locking disk, and a lid liner. Lay the acetate disk over the right side of your work and center it by counting how many empty blocks show under the acetate. Make sure that you have the same number of unworked blocks at the top as you have at the bottom, and an equal number on each side. Mark

around the edge of the acetate with a pencil to form a cutting line (see p. 99, Step 8).

Cut out the embroidery along the cutting line, then place the acetate disk into the lid, followed by the embroidery, then the sponge disk. Check that the embroidery is correctly displayed and then push home the metal locking plate. Finally, add the lid liner, holding it in place with a little glue if necessary.

Coasters

To display your work in a coaster, first back the embroidery with iron-on interfacing to prevent fraying. Center the backing plate of the coaster over the work and draw around it with a pencil. Cut the work out along the pencil line and place it in the coaster. Push home the backing plate to finish. The results can be seen in the photograph on page 108.

Paperweights

Attractive paperweights can be bought in which to display cross stitch designs. When the embroidery is

A simple heart design has been used in different ways and with different colors for these items (see chart, p. 113). A 2½ x 2¼in (6.5 x 5.5cm) heart-shaped paperweight frames a pastel version of the design. Work with care on cream 22-count Hardanger, as the thick glass of the paperweight magnifies the stitching slightly, so every twist on the thread will show. The same heart design has been worked in primary colors over waste canvas to add a special touch to a pair of children's jeans. Always test selected threads for colorfastness (see p.109).

complete, back with iron-on interfacing. Lay the paper disk (supplied with the paperweight) on a dark surface or against a window during daylight. Center the embroidery right side up on top of the disk, which will show through the work. Pencil the outline of the disc onto the fabric. Cut out and place the design in the paperweight. Place the paper disk over the back of the embroidery and cover with the sticky backing disk (which can be repositioned if necessary).

WALL HANGINGS

Some designs, particularly long, narrow ones, can be mounted successfully as wall hangings. This avoids the need for a frame or mat. However, the work is exposed to dust and will need to be removed from its mounts and washed periodically (p. 109). Bell-pull ends are used to support the work. These are available in many sizes and finishes.

Lamb Wall Hanging

As an alternative to framing the work in a card mount, the lamb design from the Birth Announcement (p. 85) can be mounted onto 3in (7.5cm) wooden bell-pull ends to make a miniature wall hanging.

Cut a piece of 6½ x 10in (16.5 x 25.5cm) white 28-count Jobelan, and work the design centered. When the stitching is complete, fold the work in half, right sides together. Stitch the seam, allowing ½in (1.25cm) seam allowance (see diagram below left). Turn right side out so that the seam is at the back, then press carefully (p. 30). Neaten the top and bottom, fold 1in (2.5cm) over the top bell-pull end and slipstitch into place at the back of the work. Repeat with the bottom of the hanging (see diagram below right). Stitch a pretty braid across the front of the work to disguise any slipstitching.

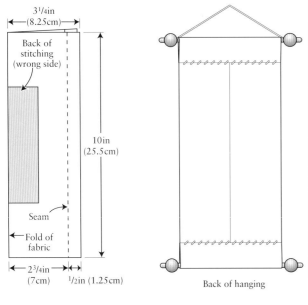

3¼in (8.25cm)

Back of stitching (wrong side)

10in (25.5cm)

Seam

Fold of fabric

2¾in (7cm)   ½in (1.25cm)

Back of hanging

GREETING CARDS

Small designs can look wonderful worked as greeting cards and are guaranteed to be treasured by the recipients. Commercial three-fold cards are available in many sizes and colors and with a wide variety of shaped openings. These are ideal for mounting embroidery, as they have a flap that covers the back of the work neatly. Check that the design you have chosen will fit into the mount you intend to use (p. 12). To mount work in a card, follow the step-by-step instructions on pages 88–89. Adapting an existing design is easy, as shown by the Valentine card on page 66, which uses the Treasure Box design. The Zodiac card on page 97 takes one of the astrological designs and makes a feature of it.

Wedding Card

By working the Wedding Picture design on page 81 on a fine fabric, the size has been reduced sufficiently to fit into a card mount (see p. 80). Remember that designs worked on fabrics with a high thread/block/HPI count will be smaller than if worked on a low count fabric (see fabric samples, pp. 9 and 11).

Work on cream 36-count Edinburgh linen, to fit a ready-made card mount with a Gothic arch-shaped opening approximately 5½ x 3in (14 x 7.5cm). Trim the finished embroidery with a small ribbon bow and a pair of miniature gold-colored horseshoes positioned at the top of the design. Mount the work into the card (p. 88) but apply double-sided tape to the inside of the opening, as shown in the diagram below.

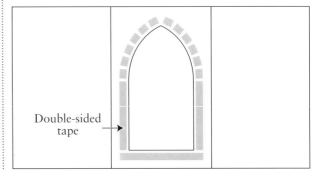

Double-sided tape

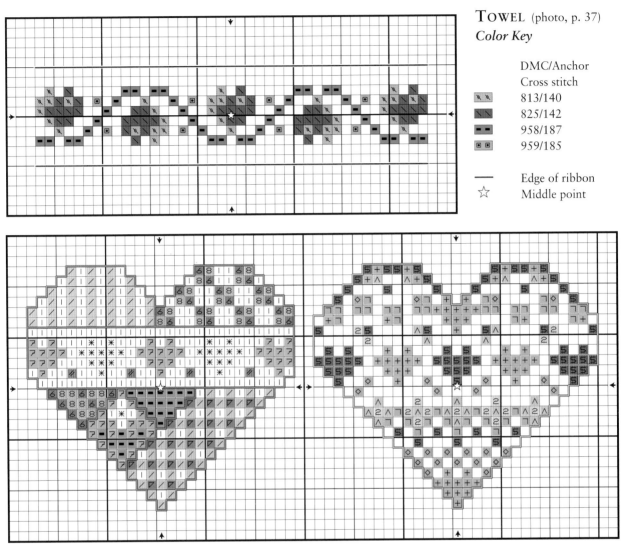

TOWEL (photo, p. 37)
Color Key

DMC/Anchor
Cross stitch

813/140
825/142
958/187
959/185

— Edge of ribbon
☆ Middle point

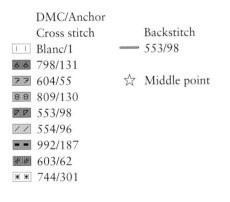

PAPERWEIGHT (photo, p. 111)
Color Key

DMC/Anchor
Cross stitch   Backstitch

Blanc/1	—	553/98
798/131		
604/55	☆	Middle point
809/130		
553/98		
554/96		
992/187		
603/62		
744/301		

HEART-SHAPED PORCELAIN BOWL (photo, p. 74)
Color Key

DMC/Anchor
Cross stitch   Backstitch

503/875	—	3726/1018
676/891		
3726/1018	☆	Middle point
3752/1032		
3727/1016		
3042/870		

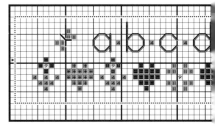

NAPKIN HOLDERS
(photos, pp. 68 & 71)

Color Key

DMC/Anchor
Cross stitch

⊓⊓	995/410
— —	554/96
I I	992/187
1 1	Blanc/1
═ ═	321/9046
⊞⊞	603/62
∥∥	699/923
⊠⊠	744/301
✳✳	726/295

—— Cutting lines

☆ Middle point

RULER (photo, p. 41)
Color Key

DMC/Anchor
Cross stitch

⊇⊇	Blanc/1	∥∥	798/131
3 3	310/403	═ ═	321/9046
4 4	699/923	⊞⊞	3607/87
5 5	400/351	H H	333/119
9 9	726/295		

Backstitch

—— 310/403 .... Cutting line
—— 321/9046 ☆ Middle point

2   1   2   3   4   5

← Repeat to row 13

Lace

PORCELAIN BOWL (photo, p. 71)
Color Key

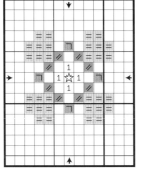

DMC/Anchor
Cross stitch

⊓⊓	340/118
1 1	Blanc/1
═ ═	3609/85
∥∥	959/186
✳✳	744/301
☆	Middle point

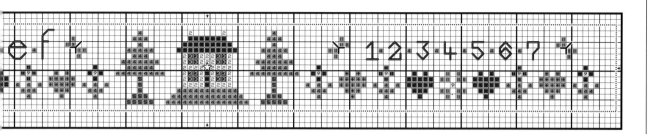

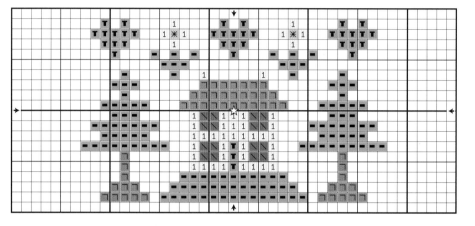

KEY TAG (photo, p. 41)
Color Key

	DMC/Anchor Cross stitch
⊓⊓	781/309
1 1	Ecru/926
⟍⟍	3768/779
▬▬	502/876
✳✳	833/907
T T	356/1013

☆　　Middle point

TARTAN CHRISTMAS FRAME
(photo, p. 107)
Color Key

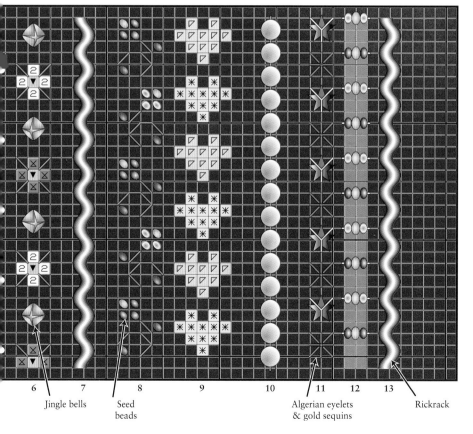

	DMC/Anchor Cross stitch
2 2	Blanc/1
▽▽	DMC light silver thread
✕✕	995/410
▮	Red fabric
→→	699/923
▦	Christmas green ribbon
✳✳	DMC light gold thread
▼▼	676/891
—	DMC light gold thread
—	699/923
—	Blanc/1
—	995/410

6   7   8   9   10   11   12   13

Jingle bells   Seed beads   Algerian eyelets & gold sequins   Rickrack

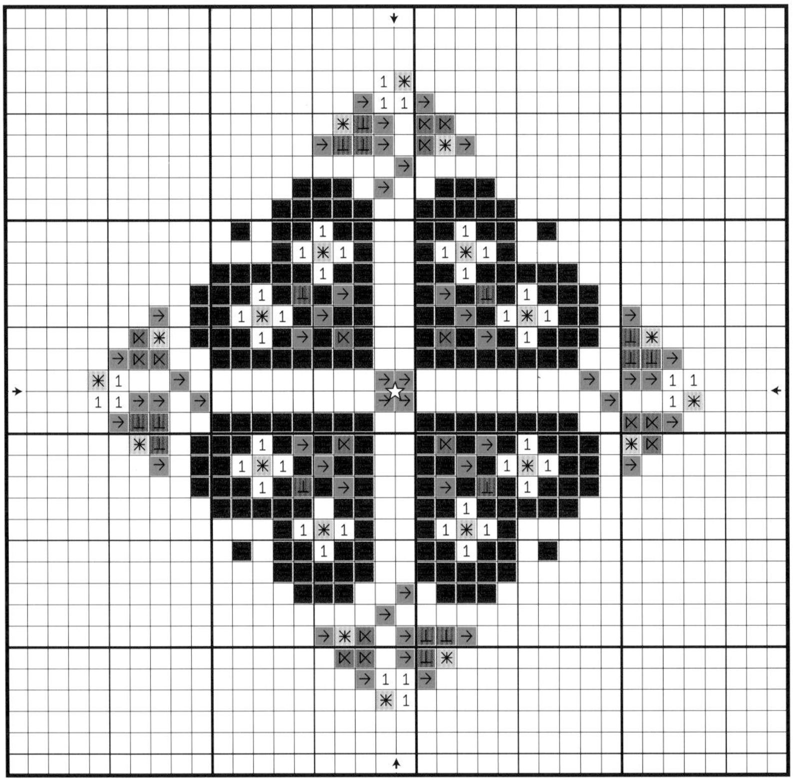

COASTER, EYEGLASS CASE & FLEXI-HOOP PICTURE (photo, p. 108)
Color Key

	DMC/Anchor Cross stitch
1 1	Blanc/1
■	321/9046
✕✕	995/410
⊥⊥	3607/87
→→	699/923
✳✳	726/295

☆   Middle point

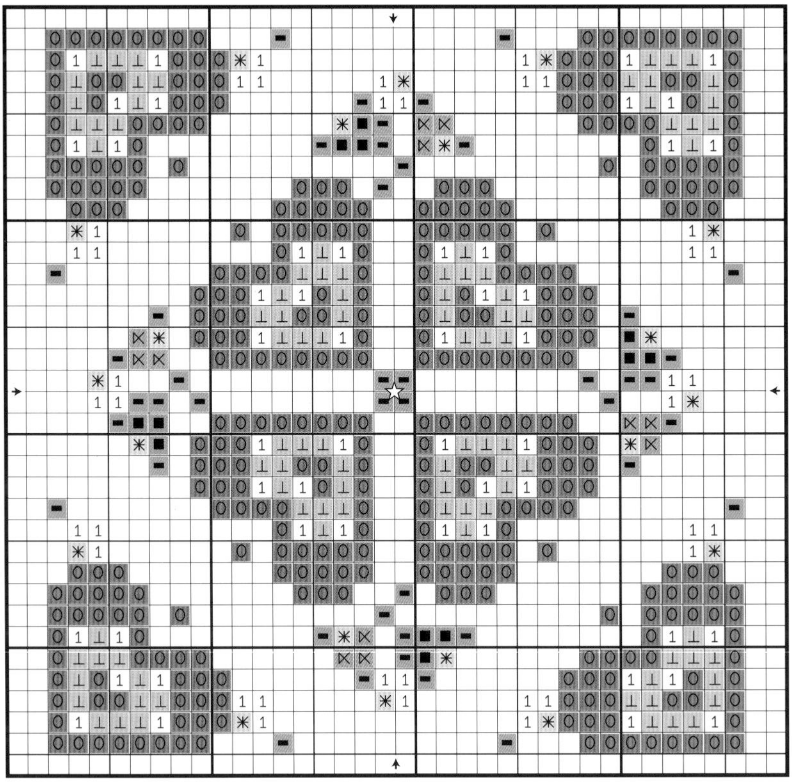

VALENTINE CARD
(photo, p. 66)
Color Key

	DMC/Anchor Cross stitch
1 1	Blanc/1
✕✕	809/130
0 0	603/62
⊥⊥	605/50
━━	992/187
✳✳	744/301
■■	554/96

☆   Middle point

THE GOLDEN RULES
OF CROSS STITCH

- Wash hands before stitching and keep work clean between embroidery sessions.

- Overcast the edges of fabric to prevent fraying.

- Work in an embroidery hoop or frame whenever possible.

- Keep all top stitches lying in the same direction.

- Do not allow twists to develop on the thread.

- Do not jump thread across the back of bare fabric.

- Trim all ends neatly, close to the fabric.

- Cut embroidery thread only with embroidery scissors.

- Do not use knots to start or finish a thread.

- Work in good light and check work frequently for mistakes.

- Never fold your work, always roll it to avoid stubborn creases.

- Press finished embroidery face down on a thick, white terry towel to avoid crushing the stitches.

Fabric	Needle size	No. of strands
6-count Binca	20	6
8-count Aida	22	4
11-count Aida	24	3
14-count Aida	26	2
16-count Aida	26	2
18-count Aida	26/28	2
20-count Bellana	24	3
22-count Oslo	24	3

Fabric	Needle size	No. of strands
25-count Dublin	24	3
27-count Linda	26	2
28-count Quaker cloth	26	2
28-count Jobelan	26	2
32-count Belfast	26	2
36-count Edinburgh	26/28	2
55-count Kingston	28	1

NOTE Add an extra strand of embroidery floss to the needle if the tension of your stitching does not give sufficient coverage of the fabric.

ACKNOWLEDGMENTS

I am yet again indebted to my stalwart band of stitchers who so willingly and expertly stitched most of the worked samples. For once the projects were mercifully small, but my gratitude is as great as ever. A big thank-you therefore to Win Barry (towel), Audrey Bryan (pincushion basket [step-by-steps]), Carol Burr (Zodiac bowl lid and card), Eileen Callender (birth announcement card), Hazel Evans (key tag, napkin holders, porcelain bowl lid), Ros Foster (blue needle case), Margaret Jones (bookmark, magnetic note holder), Sandra Kedzlie (eyeglass case), Elizabeth Lovesey (flexi-hoop picture), Edna McCready (white needle case), Sue Moir (Valentine card), Sue Moore (wedding card), Sylvia Morgan (family tree picture), Val Morgan (chatelaine), Penny Peberdy (heart-shaped bowl lid, paperweight), Jenny Potts (a First Sampler), Ann Sansom (lamb wall hanging), Linda Smith (coaster), Christine Thomas (pincushion basket), Nancy Verso (wedding picture), Irene Vincent (ruler), Jenny Way (Christmas heart-shaped baskets).

Many thanks also to Cheryl Brown, Brenda Morrison, and Lin Clements at David & Charles for all their help; to Jane Trollope, who lent both hands for the step-by-step photographs; to Ethan Danielson, who sorted out the charts with such patience; and to David and Kit Johnson and Alan Duns for the sparkling photographs.

I am grateful to the following suppliers for their generous assistance in the production of this book:

Cara Ackerman at DMC Creative World Ltd, Alastair McMinn & Steph Thannhaüser at Coats Patons Crafts, Mike Gray at Framecraft Miniatures Ltd, R & P Sperr at S & A Frames, Gillian Leeper at Spoilt for Choice, Beryl Lee at Artisan, Voirrey Branthwaite at The Voirrey Embroidery Centre, Helen Kirkup at The Campden Needlecraft Centre, JRM Beads, Jenny Kearley at Craft Creations Ltd, Jane Greenoff at Jane Greenoff's Inglestone Collection, Judy Raine at Janet Coles Beads, Ian and Martin Lawson Smith at IL-Soft, Carole Morris at Spangles, Tony and Wendy Foster at Warwick Studios, and John Lewis.

INDEX